XVII
28

$2·75

D1180757

MAGIC
OF THE MASTERS

Jack Delvin
MAGIC
OF THE MASTERS

with special artwork by
The Hayward Art Group

HAMLYN
London · New York · Sydney · Toronto

Published by
The Hamlyn Publishing Group Limited
London · New York · Sydney · Toronto
Astronaut House, Feltham, Middlesex, England

© Copyright The Hamlyn Publishing Group Limited 1977
ISBN 0 600 36238 8

Filmset in England by Keyspools, Golborne, Lancashire
Printed in England by Sackville Smeets, Billericay

CONTENTS

The Return of
THE
YELLOW PERILS

'Take two identical horses' – that was my introduction to the literature of magic. Not a lot of use to a young man of six. Unfortunately most magic books are written for the merely curious, not for those who genuinely wish to learn the art. There's a lot of difference between knowing how to do a trick and being able to present it successfully before an audience.

The utter impossibility of my getting hold of one horse, let alone two identical horses, almost changed the whole course of my life – out of magic, not into it. Then I discovered 'The Yellow Perils', a series of little yellow-backed books published in the early 1900s at two shillings (10p or 20c) and containing detailed instructions on how to perform the tricks of the master magicians with objects I could easily get hold of like cards and coins and things. That was it; the magic bug bit me and I've stayed bitten ever since.

I found out later that it was the professional magicians who had branded these books 'The Yellow Perils'. And the reason? They contained so many top secrets that the magicians of the day feared their publication would wreck the profession. After all, isn't the main law of magic 'Never tell your secrets'? And here were the top secrets of master magicians like David Devant, Howard Thurston, T. Nelson Downs, and Charles Bertram for all the world to see – and learn.

For nearly fifty years these invaluable little books have been out of print. Now they are collector's items and change hands for as much as £10 ($20) each. Today the tricks they describe are common currency, performed wherever magicians set out to entertain. Wouldn't it, I thought, be a good idea to select the best of these perennial favourites and present them in the modern idiom? So here they are – 'The Magic of the Masters' or 'The Return of the Yellow Perils'. Why? To celebrate a great and lasting event in the literature of magic. And because, like David Devant and a great many other professional magicians, I learned my magic from books and hope to help others become master

8

magicians too. Why shouldn't *you* give it a try?

But before you begin to learn 'The Magic of the Masters', may I offer some advice? At first many of the sleights described will seem to be completely beyond your capabilities and you may well feel like giving up. Do not despair, however, as even the most accomplished of today's magicians encountered exactly the same problem when they started. Take the various moves one by one, practising each move over and over again, before tackling the next. In this way your confidence will grow, your hands will become accustomed to their new skills, and the task will seem steadily less arduous.

Once you have completely mastered the mechanics of a trick, then comes its presentation. Many of the purely manipulative routines are best performed silently, preferably to suitable musical accompaniment. Into this category come tricks like 'The Miser's Dream', card-catching routines, or the thimble routine. On the other hand, several of the tricks require you to talk, or 'patter' as it is called. The choice is yours.

If you perform silently, you will need to practise mime. That means registering exactly the right expressions on your face and making the right gestures with your hands so as to convey visually your reactions to the magic taking place. For instance, if a billiard ball suddenly appears from nowhere, your whole being should register surprise. A good mime will carry an audience along, fooling the spectators not only with manual dexterity but also with acting ability. The mime magician may be serious or amusing as befits his or her own personality. The same is also true of the 'patter merchant'. So ask yourself, 'Can I say things which make people laugh or am I a serious sort of person?'

Several of 'The Yellow Perils' included the patter to use during the performance of each of the tricks described. But, of course, styles in presentation change and the rather long-winded, stilted manner of those times would not suit modern audiences at all. The modern tendency is away from the serious, mysterious approach towards a more lighthearted, or even broad, comedy style.

Personally I am against interspersing magic with jokes that have little or no connection with the tricks. It is far better for the comedy to arise naturally from the situation created by the trick. A perfect example of this is 'The All-Change Silk', where the chagrin of the poor spectator whose handkerchief is destroyed before his very eyes will produce laughter from any audience.

Patter has several functions. It can help to create the right atmosphere, explain proceedings where necessary, entertain the audience, and provide misdirection at crucial points. Some performers studiously write out every single word of their patter, making sure that it fits exactly every tiny move to be made and, more importantly, engages the spectators' attention in order to misdirect them at precisely the right moments. But patter can arise naturally from the proceedings, and others find their patter builds up gradually over a long period of time and after numerous public performances.

In some of the tricks where patter is necessary, I have suggested the line you might use. Mostly, however, I have left the patter out altogether as what suits one performer is quite wrong for another. The presentation of magic is a totally personal matter. Success can only be achieved by first selecting the right tricks, i.e. ones suited not only to the environment in which they are to be performed, but also to the individual performer; secondly, by acquiring through constant practice the skills necessary for their accomplishment; and thirdly by presenting them in such a way as to allow the performer's own personality to shine forth. Books of jokes and patter 'angles' are readily available from magic-dealers, but remember always that patter is a very individual matter. It is one of the keystones which turn an average performer into a master magician.

Many of the moves included in this book can be performed equally well with either hand playing the leading role. In explaining some of the moves, however, I have found it necessary to assume that the reader is right-handed. I apologise to the left-handers and hope they will find no difficulty in 'translating' the instructions where necessary.

Now for the magic . . .

The famous Rising Card Trick, originated by Howard Thurston and performed here by the author, Jack Delvin

CARD MAGIC

The Principal Sleights
The two-handed pass

The most important of all sleights with playing cards is the 'pass'. This is the method by which it is possible to bring a card from the centre of a pack of cards to the top or the bottom as required. What actually happens is that the top half of the pack is transposed with the bottom half, unseen by the audience. The method for the two-handed pass given here is exactly as performed by Charles Bertram. Since its publication there have been numerous so-called improvements. Having tried out every one that has come my way, I still prefer the following.

Take the pack in your left hand as though you are going to deal. Open the cards at the place you require, usually above a selected card. Insert your little finger to keep a break at this point (Fig. 1). Bring your right hand towards the pack and at the same time relax your left hand so that the cards open as though hinged. They should be about 1 inch (2·54 cm) apart at the bottom and about 2 inches (5·08 cm) apart at the top. This will bring the top half of the pack obliquely under your right-hand fingers. With your second, third, and little fingers acting as a screen, you grasp the lower half of the pack between your forefinger and thumb (Fig. 2).

Then, with the fingers of your left hand, draw the top half downwards to clear the bottom half (Fig. 3). To assist the action, press down on the centre of the bottom half with your left thumb, thus turning this half on the pivot created by your right thumb and forefinger. This will raise the lower edge of the bottom half and enable the top half to clear it easily. As soon as it is clear, you bring the top half underneath the bottom half by closing your left fingers (Fig. 4). Square up the cards and the pass is complete.

This sleight must be practised over and over again in front of a mirror until it becomes one instantaneous, noiseless movement. It should be completely invisible to the

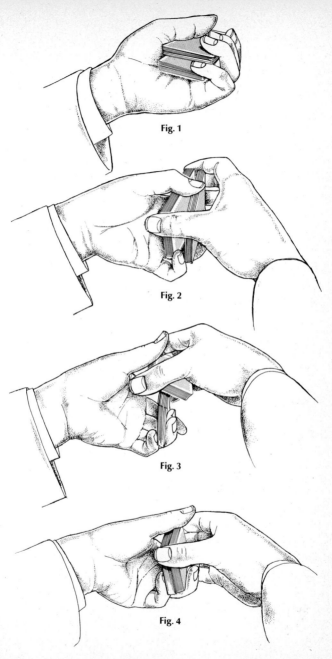

Fig. 1

Fig. 2

Fig. 3

Fig. 4

audience as the whole action is screened by your right hand. For the sake of clarity the diagrams greatly exaggerate the distances between the two halves of the pack. In fact they slide around each other and the audience sees only the back of your right hand throughout.

The one-handed pass

Originally the 'Charlier Pass', the method given here incorporates improvements by Charles Bertram.

Hold the pack in your left hand, faces towards the audience, with the point of your thumb on a level with the edge of the pack. Your little finger must be kept at the bottom of the pack to make a rest. Your second and third fingers must be holding the pack tightly opposite your thumb. At this stage your forefinger should be free, touching the pack only to help square it up before the movement (Fig. 5).

By slightly raising the ball of your thumb, release the top half of the pack so that it drops into your palm (Fig. 6). With your free forefinger, push the top half upwards until it reaches the upper edge of the lower half, making a tent-like shape. Your thumb prevents the top half of the pack from going too far (Fig. 7). Now, by slightly opening your hand, the lower half will fall onto your forefinger, which gently lowers it, allowing your thumb to slide the upper half over the falling cards. You can then grip the pack in all your fingers and square it up.

These movements should blend smoothly so, as the top half drops (Fig. 6), slightly lower your hand, and at the moment of making the final move (Fig. 7), the cards should be brought towards your body with a sweeping gesture and away again, placing the faces of the cards towards the audience at the end.

This description of Charles Bertram's one-handed pass is based upon his own performance of the sleight. Apparently he used it in order to cause a visible change of the front card. If this sleight is to be used for the more common

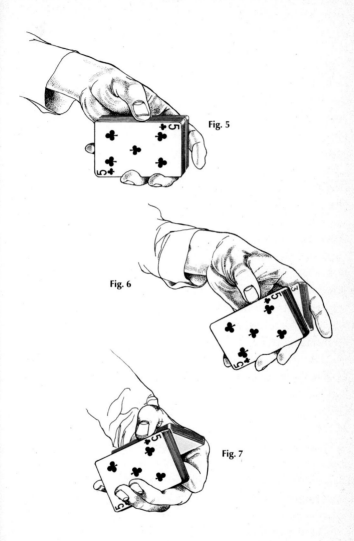

Fig. 5

Fig. 6

Fig. 7

object of bringing a selected card to the top or bottom of the pack, then the cards must be faced away from your audience. Various ways of locating the selected card are given in this chapter.

The palm from the top of the pack

Of almost equal importance to the pass is the 'palm'. Sleight of hand is made up of various dexterous skills and moves by which means small objects can be made to appear and disappear at will. The basis of most sleights is the ability to conceal a small object in the hand whilst it appears to be empty, and this sleight is known as 'palming'. There are many different ways of palming and several are explained in this book. Once again we turn first to Charles Bertram for his method.

In all sleight of hand it is of extreme importance to learn this rule: the hand that secretly takes an object should not immediately move with it! The fact of a hand moving towards an object and then being removed without being shown empty suggests that something has been taken. In developing his method, Charles Bertram eliminated this error, which had been apparent in all descriptions of the palm until then.

Take the cards in your left hand as though about to deal. Bring your right hand towards the pack and place your four fingers on the top edge. With your right thumb lift up the top card, and at the same time insert your left little finger into the opening caused at the bottom edge. Bend the card by squeezing your right thumb and fingers together slightly, thus making the card bow outwards somewhat. At exactly the same moment, move your left hand, containing the pack, away from your right and with your left second finger give the card a sudden poke which will make it spring into the palm. *Do not take the right hand away from the left*. The fact that the left hand leaves the right misdirects your audience into thinking your right hand is still empty.

Because the palm is so important I have had the whole sequence covered very fully with diagrams. First is the position of the cards in the left hand as the right approaches (Fig. 8). The next shows the right hand just grasping the card to be palmed at either end between fingers and thumb while the left thumb helps to bridge the card (Fig. 9). Then

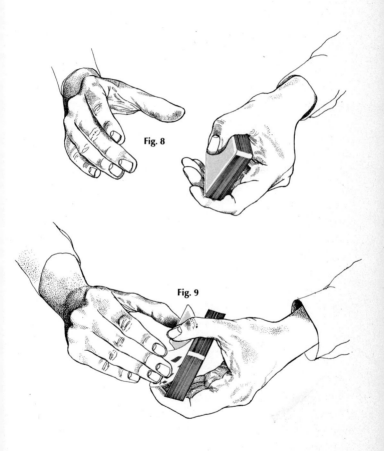

Fig. 8

Fig. 9

we see the left hand holding the pack about to move away (Fig. 10); and the same stage from a different angle so that you can see the position more clearly (Fig. 11). In the next diagram the left hand moves away a little with the pack, and the second finger is inserted between the pack and the bridged card (Fig. 12), ready to push it into the palm with a sharp touch at the centre (Fig. 13). Then the card is shown safe in the right palm and the left hand moves the pack away (Fig. 14). The left hand has completed its action but the right hand has not moved at all.

Obviously all these diagrams have been drawn from a side angle. From the audience's point of view all that happens is the right hand moves to the pack simply to square the cards, and when this has been done the left hand moves the pack away.

Very often, having palmed a card, it is necessary to pass the pack to a member of your audience to be shuffled. Do not do this with your left hand. It is far better to take the pack between the fingers and thumb of your right hand and then hand it out. This is a far more natural move and will allay all suspicion that a card could be concealed in the hand.

This method is so controlled that it is possible to palm several cards off the pack simultaneously.

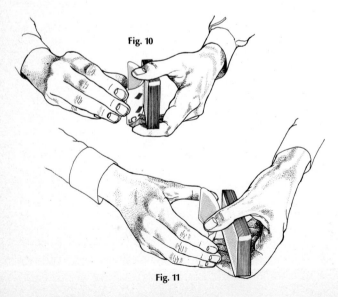

Fig. 10

Fig. 11

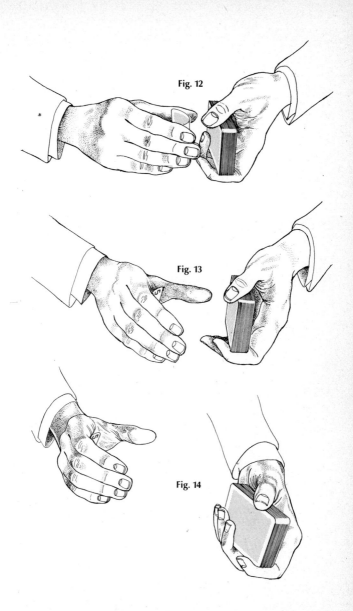

Fig. 12

Fig. 13

Fig. 14

The palm from the bottom of the pack

Hold the pack in your left hand. Move your right hand as though to square the cards. With the forefinger of your left hand, slide the bottom card forward until its edge reaches the 'padded' parts of the first phalanges of your right-hand fingers. Withdraw the rest of the pack with your left thumb, second, third, and fourth fingers (Fig. 15). Meantime you continue to press on the card with your left forefinger until it is wholly in the right hand and the pack is clear. Move your left hand containing the pack away, clear of your right hand. Keep the right hand still for a moment or two before dropping it to your side.

As far as your audience is concerned, all the right hand has done is square up the pack in the left hand, which has then moved the pack away in a perfectly natural manner. Of course the back of your right hand is towards the audience the whole time and completely masks the move.

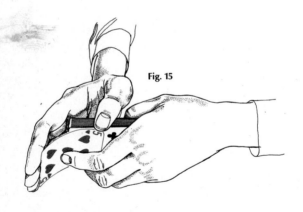

Fig. 15

The back and front palm

The description given here is the method that was used by Paul Valadon, an extremely clever card manipulator. The sleight is not used in card tricks as such, but is the basic move of those performers who appear to catch cards from

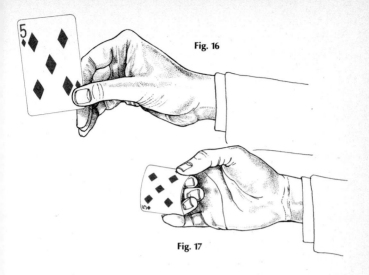

Fig. 16

Fig. 17

the air. Cardini was the greatest exponent of this type of act and many of today's performers include the production of card fans in their routines.

I suggest you limit yourself to one card at first until you have mastered the move completely. Later you may wish to increase the number until you can manipulate sufficient to enable you to produce a whole fan of cards. The effect you are aiming for is to make a chosen card disappear. You show a card held between the thumb and forefinger of either hand. With a slight upward movement of your hand you make the card vanish. You then show both sides of your hand to prove that the card is concealed neither in the palm nor at the back of your hand.

Now for the method. Take a card between your thumb and forefinger (Fig. 16). Make a slight downward movement, followed by a slight upward movement of your hand and forearm. At the same time complete this action: by moving your thumb, allow the card to fall across the back of your first, second, and third fingers and bring your little finger up to the edge of the card (Fig. 17). Grip that edge of the card

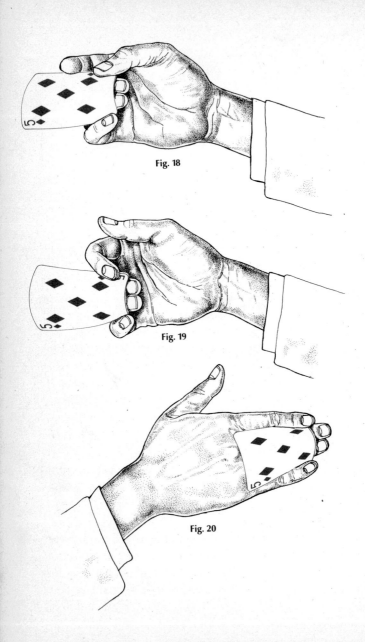

Fig. 18

Fig. 19

Fig. 20

between your little finger and your third finger, and remove your forefinger so that your thumb grips the opposite edge of the card between itself and your second finger (Fig. 18). Your forefinger must now move down the edge of the card and take the place of the thumb, gripping the edge of the card against your second finger. This allows you to move your thumb away (Fig. 19). Extend your fingers and the back palm is complete (Fig. 20). The card has disappeared and your palm is clearly empty.

Now to show the back of your hand. You turn your hand over, bringing your thumb to the front. While your hand is turning, the following action takes place. You close your fingers into your palm and grip the centre of the edge of the card with your thumb (Fig. 21). This allows you to open your four fingers outwards (Fig. 22) until your first and little fingers grip the edges of the card against your two middle fingers (Fig. 23) and, upon the completion of the turn of the hand, you show the back to the audience.

To reverse the palm once more so that you can show the front of your hand still empty, you turn your hand over again, meantime carrying out the following action. Press your thumb against the centre of the bottom edge of the card (Fig. 24). This will allow your two centre fingers to come down the back of the card and your first and little fingers to travel down the edges at the same time (Fig. 25). Continue the thumb pressure until the tips of your two centre fingers protrude from the bottom edge of the card. Now, if you press the card edges with your first and little fingers against the other two fingers and open your hand (Fig. 26), the card will be once more held securely concealed on the back of your hand.

The number of combinations of vanishes and recoveries using this sleight is legion. You can, for example, pass one card from one hand to the other and back again. Or you can take, say, five cards one at a time and make them disappear, showing your hand back and front and finally producing them as a fan.

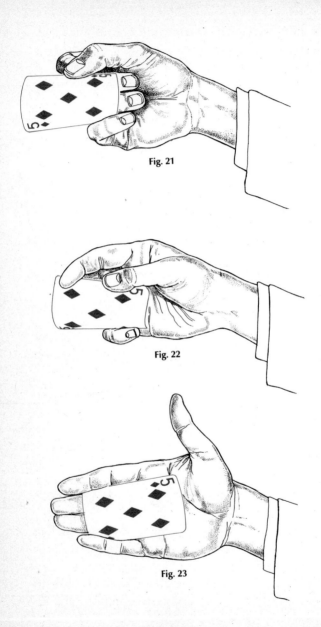

Fig. 21

Fig. 22

Fig. 23

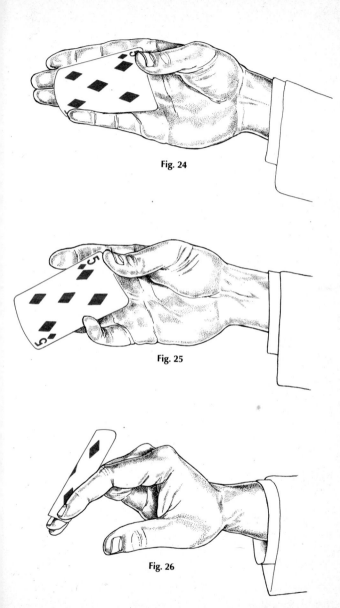

Fig. 24

Fig. 25

Fig. 26

The false shuffle

There are many ways of false shuffling a pack of cards and I give you here three different versions.

First method   This false shuffle keeps any number of cards up to, say, twenty-five in order on top of a pack.

Take the pack in your left hand, its long side at the bottom, your thumb being on the back of the top card and your fingers on the face of the bottom card. With the thumb, second, and third fingers of your right hand, grip the pack across the length at a position just below the pre-arranged cards. At the same time, slightly curve your forefinger to bring it to about the top centre of the pack on the face of the bottom card.

Now lift the portion of the pack you have gripped just clear of the pre-arranged cards (Fig. 27). As soon as this portion is clear, allow the pre-arranged stack to drop from your thumb to the fingers of your left hand, meanwhile bringing the other portion over into the position next to the thumb of your left hand (Fig. 28).

Lift your right hand, taking with it the stack of pre-arranged cards and also about half of the portion which is in front (Fig. 29). You must now shuffle the cards held by the thumb, second, and third fingers of your right hand with those remaining in the left and conclude the shuffle by leaving the pre-arranged stack, which is now behind your right forefinger (Fig. 29), on the top of the pack.

Second method   This will enable you to keep the top and bottom cards in their positions.

Proceed as with the previous method but only five or six of the top cards need be left (Fig. 27). Take care when shuffling to leave the bottom card in its position, concluding as before by placing those cards behind your forefinger (Fig. 29) onto the top of the pack, thus returning the top card to its original place.

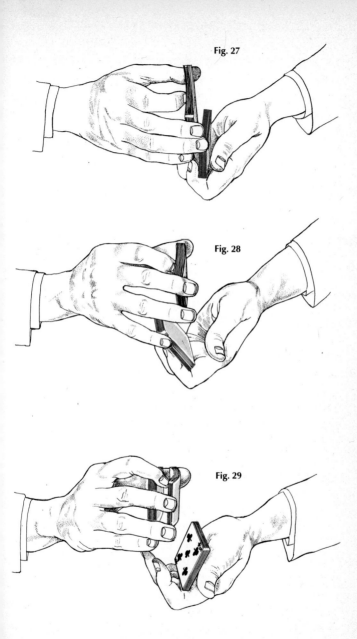

Fig. 27

Fig. 28

Fig. 29

Third method   This keeps the whole pack in a pre-arranged order, known by conjurers as a 'stacked' pack.

Take the stacked pack and follow the second method exactly as described up to the position shown in Figure 29. In the first two methods the cards now remaining in your left hand and those held between the thumb, second, and third fingers of your right hand have been fairly shuffled, although in the second method the bottom card was left in position. In this third method the cards in your left hand become very important.

Hold them loosely resting upon your fingers and, gripping the other two portions in your right hand, pretend to drop some of the portion held between your thumb, second, and third fingers upon their backs. Do not in fact release any cards, but immediately raise your right hand, at the same time tossing the cards in your left hand over with your fingers onto the thumb to expose their faces. Now drop a few of the cards from your right thumb, second, and third fingers onto these, taking care not to change their order. Immediately push the cards in your left hand over onto the fingers with your thumb and again simulate the movement of leaving some cards with your right hand. Toss the cards back onto your left thumb and once more visibly drop some cards upon the face of those held in your left hand.

This action is continued until the cards held between your right thumb, second, and third fingers are used up. Then drop the portion remaining behind your forefinger in one go upon the backs of the cards in your left hand. The shuffle has been completed without rearranging a single card. Throughout the whole of this false shuffle the cards in your left hand must be kept moving backwards and forwards by your thumb and fingers to achieve the best effect.

Forcing a card

'To force a card' means to make a spectator take the card from the pack that you wish to be chosen. There are numerous ways of performing this, but the classic 'fan force' is without doubt the best and most natural. It is, of course, essential that the choice appears to be absolutely free.

First you must note the name of the bottom card and by means of the pass bring it to the centre of the pack, keeping a break with your little finger between the two halves. Hold the pack face downwards between both hands, thumbs on the backs of the cards and fingers below; now spread the cards like a fan from left to right and bring them towards the chooser. As the spectator puts out a hand to select a card, move about ten to fifteen of the centre cards by passing your left thumb from left to right.

You must time this movement so that just as the chooser's fingers reach the pack the card you wish to force comes between them. Take your time over this, remembering that the choice must appear to be completely free and that this is aided by the passing of the cards from left to right in front of the chooser's hand. You must vary the speed at which you pass the cards in accordance with how quickly or slowly the hand is put out to take one.

In using this force, it is essential that you have an 'out' in the event that the wrong card is selected. In my opinion it is far better to allow the wrong card to be taken than to run the risk of revealing your desire for one particular card to be chosen. If the wrong card is selected, just pass on to a second spectator, retaining your break, and force the correct card. Deal with the first card by performing some small trick, and then move to the second spectator and perform the trick for which it was necessary to force the card in the first place.

Easy Card Tricks
The Turned Card

In this trick the magician has a card selected and re-placed. Then, when the pack is spread on the table, it is seen that all the cards are face downwards apart from one card, the chosen one, which has turned itself upwards.

With the pack of cards backs upwards, slide your left little finger beneath the top card and make the two-handed pass, but bring the card to the bottom face upwards. This means that every card in the pack is face downwards apart from the bottom card, which is face upwards.

Fan the cards before the spectator, making sure that the bottom card is unseen, and ask the person to take one. As soon as a card has been taken, secretly turn the pack over and carefully, keeping the cards squared up, ask the spectator to replace the card by pushing it anywhere into the pack. Since the top card is reversed, the impression is that all the cards are backs upwards. In fact only two cards are backs up, the top card and the chosen card.

Slide your little finger beneath the top card again and pass it round the pack to the bottom, reversing it once more. Place the pack on the table face down and ask for the card to be named, explaining that you will cause the chosen card to reveal itself. Quickly spread out the cards along the table and the chosen card will be clearly seen amongst the others, face up.

Catching Two Cards

This is quite a startling little trick and very easy to do. Two cards are chosen, replaced, and shuffled into the pack. The magician takes the pack, throws it into the air, and plunging a hand amongst the falling cards catches the chosen two.

Two cards are chosen and, whilst your back is turned, have them shown to the audience. When the first card is replaced into the pack, make a break above it with your left little finger, and perform the pass to bring it to the top. Have the second card replaced in the centre of the pack, again keeping a break above it with your left little finger. This card must be slid to the bottom of the pack and this is very easily accomplished. In addition to the little finger, push your forefinger into the break so that it too is resting

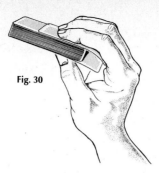

Fig. 30

upon the chosen card. Now using these two fingers, slide the chosen card downwards out of the pack under cover of the right-hand fingers and move it to the bottom. (This, of course, is almost a version of the pass.)

Perform a false shuffle, keeping the top and bottom cards in position, and then take the pack in your right hand, fingers on the backs and the thumb on the faces. Throw the pack into the air, removing the top and bottom cards (Fig. 30) and instantly plunging your hand into the falling cards as though catching the two chosen cards from amongst them.

It adds greatly to the effect if you are able to glimpse the indexes of the two cards when you transfer them to the top and bottom of the pack respectively as this enables you to call their names before you catch them.

The Artful Card

A card is chosen and shuffled back into the pack. The magician hides the pack behind him or her and claims to be able to find the chosen card immediately. So saying, a card is produced but it is the wrong one. The magician asks the chooser to name the card and takes this very card from a coat pocket.

To perform this surprising little trick, hand the pack to someone for shuffling and ask that one card be removed and shown to the audience. Have the card replaced but, by means of the pass, bring it to the top of the pack and false shuffle. Now place the cards behind your back and palm off the chosen top card; then remove the next card from the pack between your right forefinger and thumb and bring it forward, claiming that it is the chosen card.

The spectators will be quick to tell you that you are wrong. Feign surprise and ask for the chosen card to be named. Upon being told the name, say that you find it difficult to understand as that particular card has been in your pocket all the time. Saying this, you insert your right hand into a coat pocket and withdraw the palmed card.

The Card through a Handkerchief Trick

This is one of my favourite impromptu card tricks. A card is selected and returned to the pack. The pack is shuffled and then wrapped up in a large pocket handkerchief. Holding the ends of the handkerchief in one hand, the magician shakes it up and down and the chosen card is seen to emerge slowly from the pack, passing right

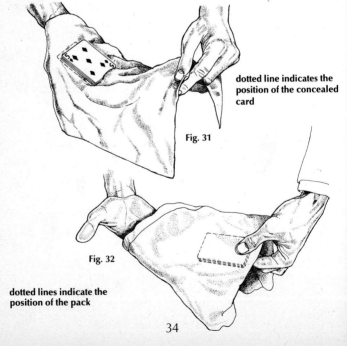

dotted line indicates the position of the concealed card

Fig. 31

Fig. 32

dotted lines indicate the position of the pack

through the handkerchief, until it falls completely clear of it.

Have any card selected and replaced. If you fan the cards and hold them fairly tightly, the spectator will not be able to push the card squarely into the pack. This will give you the opportunity to make a break above the chosen card and bring it to the top by means of the pass. While the handkerchief is being examined, palm off the chosen card in your right hand and, when you receive the handkerchief again, immediately drape it over this hand.

Now pass the cards out for shuffling. On their return, place them face upwards upon the centre of the handkerchief, immediately over the palmed card (Fig. 31). Fold the front half of the handkerchief back over the pack. Take hold of the pack in your left hand, together with the hidden chosen card (Fig. 32). Gather up the loose ends of the handkerchief on either side of the pack and bring them upwards at the back, trapping the chosen card in the folds (Fig. 33 and 34). If you now give the handkerchief a gentle shake, the chosen card will gradually make its appearance (Fig. 35).

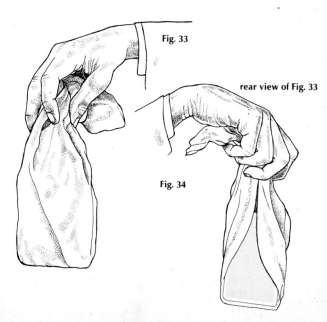

Fig. 33

rear view of Fig. 33

Fig. 34

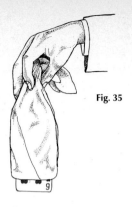

Fig. 35

Card manipulations

The production of fans of cards using the back palm is very popular with magicians. Various other manipulations are often included to give variety. Here are two in which the magician takes three or four cards in the right hand and transfers them to the left hand, from which they disappear.

First method Fan the cards in your right hand as shown in the diagram (Fig. 36) and then let them drop into your palm (Fig. 37). Now bring your right hand up to the left as though transferring them (Fig. 38). In fact, helped by your left-hand fingers, they are palmed in your right hand (Fig. 39). Immediately close your left hand partially as though it contained the cards and turn its back to the audience. Pass

Fig. 36

Fig. 37

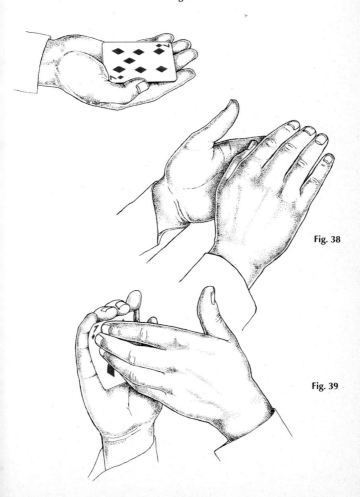

Fig. 38

Fig. 39

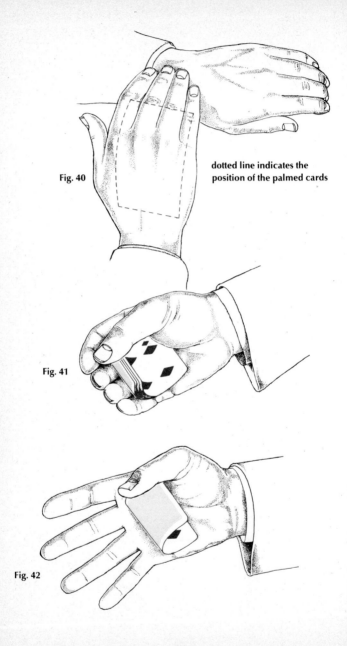

Fig. 40

dotted line indicates the position of the palmed cards

Fig. 41

Fig. 42

your right hand across the back of your left hand from right to left from your wrist to your fingertips as though drawing the cards through the left hand by magnetism (Fig. 40).

Now comes a neat move. Grasp the corners of the cards with your right thumb and bend them into the palm of your hand (Figs. 41 and 42). This enables you to pass your right hand across the back of your left hand again but this time with your fingers open. Drop your right hand casually to your side and slowly turn your left hand round to show it empty. Reproduce the cards as a fan from behind your right knee.

Second method Hold the cards between your right fore-finger and thumb and pass your left hand across the front of your right hand as though taking them (Fig. 43). Under cover of your left hand, quickly back palm them behind your right hand (Fig. 44). The audience expect to see you

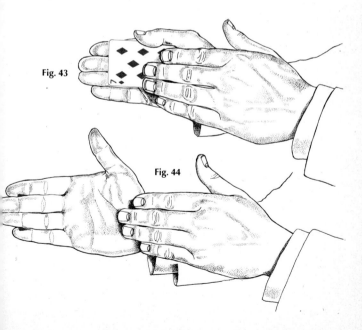

Fig. 43

Fig. 44

produce them from your left hand and are therefore surprised when you turn this hand to the front and show that it is empty too. With practice the cards can then be produced one at a time at the fingertips of your right hand and the routine continued as desired.

The Reversed Card

This must be one of the easiest of all card tricks. Three picture cards are placed face upwards in a row and a member of the audience is asked to reverse one of them while the performer's back is turned. This is done, and one glance is sufficient to enable the magician to name the reversed card.

If you examine the court cards, you will find that the white margin is frequently narrower on one side than the other. Choose three such cards and when you place them down in a row, just make sure that all the narrow sides are towards the right. The card that has been turned will be the only card with its narrow margin on the left.

A Tale with a Twist

From a pack of cards take the four kings, queens, knaves, and aces. You will also need four common cards from each of the four suits. First you lay the four queens face upwards in a row, and then tell this story:

'Once upon a time four queens decided to leave their courts to dig for diamonds. (Place the four diamond-suit cards half over the queens.) Each had a spade. (Put a common spade half over each of the diamonds.) The kings sent their champions to protect them. (Put the four aces half over the spades.) But, still not satisfied that their queens would be safe, the kings set out too. (Place the kings half over the aces.) Despite all this protection, four robbers (place out the four knaves), each with a big club (place out the common clubs), waited in hiding for the queens' return, meaning to steal the diamonds. Although the robbers were absolute villains, they had brave hearts (place out the four common hearts) and were ready to face all odds in their attempt to steal the treasure.'

All the cards are now laid out neatly on the table in four columns. Take up the left-hand column, pushing the cards together into a heap but making sure that you keep them in order, and then place them face downwards on the table. Treat the remaining three columns in the same way, placing the heaps face downwards upon each other. Now give the cards to be cut as many times as your audience wish, providing each person makes a single cut and replaces it each time. When this has been completed, you proceed to lay the cards out again in columns and, lo and behold, they are in the same order as they were at the end of the story. It seems impossible that all the cutting has not disturbed the arrangement, but such is the case. All you have to do is let the spectators cut the cards until a common heart comes to the bottom.

The Four Burglars

The four jacks from a pack are shown and the magician says that they are to represent four burglars, while the pack will act as a house that is to be burgled. The four jacks are placed on top of the pack, which is arranged face down.

Continuing the story, the magician declares that one burglar was put on watch; the top jack is taken from the pack and placed in full view very close to it. Another went into the basement; the next card is taken from the top and placed into the pack very near the bottom. A third burglar went to the ground floor to see what he could find in the living and dining rooms; card number three is taken from the top of the pack and placed about the middle. Finally, the last burglar chose the bedrooms to plunder; the fourth card is removed and put into the pack very near the top.

Suddenly the burglar on watch sees a policeman coming. He rushes to the house, climbs up a drain pipe onto the

41

roof, and shouts the alarm to his comrades. Quick as a flash they join him on the roof and escape into the night. The magician places the jack who was 'on watch' on top of the pack and, to the audience's amazement, proceeds to remove the four jacks one at a time from the top of the pack where they are once again assembled.

Unknown to the audience, you hide three indifferent cards behind the third jack. This means that, when the cards are placed on top of the pack, they are in order from the top: jack, three indifferent cards, three jacks. Of course the three extra cards must be held perfectly squared-up behind the third jack. If they are held correctly, it should be possible to show the cards in a fan, on both sides, without the extra cards being detected.

Close the fan and place the cards face downwards on top of the pack in keeping with the story. The top card is a jack, so this can be removed and shown, before being placed on guard. The next three cards are indifferent cards and can be lost in the pack quite happily, leaving the three jacks intact on top awaiting the finale. Of course you must take care not to show the faces of the three indifferent cards as you put them into their positions. Given this care, and neatness in handling the phoney fan, you will find 'The Four Burglars' an extremely successful and well-received trick.

The One-Ahead Card

A spectator is asked to cut the pack into three heaps. The magician then proceeds to name the top cards without looking at them. Just in case the audience thinks it's a fluke, the magician repeats the effect with equal success.

Secretly you must note the names of the top two cards. That's right, only two. You don't need to know any more. Say they are the ten of hearts and three of clubs. When the pack has been cut into three, take care to see where the top third lands; you know that the top card of this section is the ten of hearts. Name this card but pick up the top card from one of the other sections, look at it, and smile as though you are correct. Suppose it is the ace of clubs; name this card before picking up the top card on the next heap. Once more smile and the audience will assume that you have named it correctly. Suppose this is the five of diamonds; state that the top card of the remaining heap is the five of diamonds, pick it up, look at it, and smile. You will of course be holding the ten of hearts, which completes the trio. You now throw down the three cards face upwards apparently in the order in which they were predicted, naming them aloud: the ten of hearts, the ace of clubs, and the five of diamonds.

If you wish to repeat the exercise, it is a simple matter as you already know that the top card of one of the heaps is the three of clubs, the card that was originally second from the top.

The Card in the Mind

Although this trick is brought about by very simple mathematics, the method is nicely hidden by a subtle spot of falsification.

The magician sorts some cards from a shuffled pack into three heaps upon the table. Stating that he or she has made three heaps of ten cards each, a member of the audience is asked to choose any pile. Having done so, the volunteer is then asked to look at the cards and mentally select any one card. The choices of heap and card are completely free.

The spectator is then asked to shuffle the cards in the chosen pile so that no one could possibly know the whereabouts of the chosen card. The chosen heap is then placed between the other two and the cards dealt into three heaps again. The magician declares the intention of trying to read the name of the chosen card in the mind of the spectator, but adds that as it is such a difficult under-taking the card will have to be impressed into the specta-tor's mind three times.

The magician picks up each of the three heaps in turn and, taking care not to see the faces of the cards, fans them towards the spectator. All the spectator has to do is take the heap the card is now in, give it a shuffle, and place it between the other two heaps. So much for the second impression.

The magician says that a suitable time must elapse between each impression of the card upon the brain so the cards must be mixed up once more. So saying, the magician again deals the cards into three heaps. Picking up each heap in turn and fanning it out, the magician asks, 'Is your card in this heap?' When the chosen card has been located, the spectator is asked to remove it and place it face downwards on the table. However, this should be done when the magician's back is turned as he or she does not want to see the card. When the action is completed, the magician names the chosen card.

As already revealed, this trick really 'works itself' mathematically. But, in order to obscure the principle from particularly astute spectators, you use magician's licence and tell a 'fib'. There are not ten cards in each heap. In actual fact, twenty-seven cards are used in all, making nine cards in each pile. If you follow the routine as described but with twenty-seven cards, taking care when dealing to keep the cards in sequence, the chosen one will inevitably wind up as the centre card of the final chosen heap. Although you state that you do not wish to see the faces of the cards, and this is true most of the time, when the heap containing the chosen card is picked out on the third occasion you must get a surreptitious 'peek' at the central, freely chosen card.

The Disappearing Ace

Three of the four aces from a pack of cards are shown in a fan and named. They are the ace of clubs, the ace of diamonds, and the ace of spades. The magician takes the three aces in turn and places them into the pack: the ace

Fig. 45

of clubs is shown and pushed in flush with the other cards near the bottom; the second card, the ace of diamonds, is pushed into the middle; and the last card, the ace of spades, is shown and placed near the top.

The magician asks to be reminded which card was placed in the centre, and is told that it was the ace of diamonds. As that is the card furthest from possible interference from either above or below, that, declares the magician, is the card to be used. The ace of diamonds is then commanded to disappear. The pack is taken by a spectator and checked, but the ace of diamonds cannot be found. The magician expresses no surprise, claiming that the ace of diamonds has flown to his or her inside coat pocket. Whereupon, removing the errant card from that pocket, the performer shows it to the audience with a smile.

As with all good tricks the secret is extremely simple. A glance at the illustration (Fig. 45) is sufficient to reveal all. When the three aces are shown at the start of the trick they appear to be the cards as stated. In fact they are the ace of clubs, the ace of *hearts*, and the ace of spades. The ace of hearts appears to be the ace of diamonds because the cards are arranged in the manner demonstrated. The point of the heart should face upwards and the two black aces are so placed as to hide the lower part of the heart, showing instead a pointed shape like one end of a diamond. You will also notice that the index pip of the ace of hearts is neatly covered by a corner of the ace of spades, thus completing the deception. The real ace of diamonds is in your inside coat pocket from the beginning.

You may have noticed in my description of the effect that, although the audience was allowed to see the faces of the two black aces, the 'ace of diamonds' was not shown. This omission will not be noticed during the performance of the trick, especially if you make a particular point of the fact that the second card is being placed at the very centre of the pack. Small points like this are always missed by seemingly attentive spectators, many of whom would be prepared to swear afterwards that they actually saw the ace of diamonds before it was inserted!

The Mystical Number

Explaining that seven is a mystical number and that, as the seventh child of a seventh child, his or her magical powers are greatly heightened when the number seven is used, the magician asks for the pack to be cut into seven heaps. A member of the audience then removes the top card of any one of the heaps, notes it, and returns it to the pile. Next, in order to lose the card completely in the pack, the magician places three of the heaps below and three above the chosen heap. To lose the card still further, the pack is cut by the magician, who even allows a spectator to cut the pack once more. Surely the chosen card must be lost without trace?

Then the magician requests that the cards be spread out on the table face upwards so that every card may be seen. With back turned, the magician asks that the chosen card be removed and placed face downwards on the table. This done, he or she faces the spectator and apparently by mind reading names the card chosen.

The patter about seven being a mystical number and the seventh child of a seventh child business is all verbal misdirection, and very necessary misdirection too, as the method is so simple. All you need to know is the name of the bottom card of the pack. You can easily get a secret glimpse of this when you handle the cards just before the performance. One way is to give the cards a shuffle and take the opportunity to note the bottom card.

When the pack is cut into seven heaps, keep an eye on the heap made from the bottom cards of the pack. When a heap has been chosen, the top card noted and returned, and you are putting three of the heaps above and three below, you must make sure that the heap with your sighted card on the bottom goes on top of the chosen card. This then becomes a 'key card' which will locate the chosen card for you. Provided the pack is cut an even number of times, the two cards will not be parted.

When the cards have been spread face upwards on the table for the spectator to find the chosen card, all you do is look for the one following your key card. If the spectator selects the heap which has your key card at the bottom, simply ask that the card be replaced on top of one of the other heaps and proceed as usual.

Once more ahead

This trick makes use of the principle already employed in the 'One-Ahead Card Trick'. Nevertheless it is a good variation that the student should know, if only to demonstrate how quite different tricks may be accomplished using the same means.

The magician spreads the cards in a 'ribbon' face downwards across the table so that a margin of the back of each card is visible. The performer then claims that the amazing power of 'auto-suggestion' is about to be demonstrated and, by its means, members of the audience will be compelled to pick out specified cards. Saying that silence is necessary during the demonstration and that the cards are not to be touched with the naked hand, the magician hands someone a pencil and asks that the king of clubs be touched. The spectator touches one of the face-down cards and the magician picks this up, checks it, and apparently satisfied asks for another card. This is repeated half a dozen times, each card being placed fanwise in the magician's left hand. When the last card has been named, indicated by a spectator, and put with the others in the fan, the cards are thrown down one at a time and named to prove that the correct cards were indeed picked out.

To perform this neat little mystery you will need to know the name and location of one card. Say third from one end is the king of clubs. If you wish, you can work with a confederate who also knows the position of this card. The first card you ask for is the king of clubs. When a card has been indicated, say the two of hearts, you pick it up, look at it, and pretend that it is the king of clubs. Then you ask for the two of hearts and the one-ahead system is in full swing. When you ask your confederate to select a final named card, he or she picks out the card third from the end, the king of clubs. This completes the 'circle' and you can now show the cards.

If you prefer to work without the aid of confederates, as I do, there is still a way this trick can be accomplished. You will need an excuse for picking up the sighted card, the king of clubs, that you name first but pick up last. You say that the feat is made more difficult by the fact that you have to remember the whereabouts of every card in the pack. 'For instance,' you say, 'this is the six of spades,' naming the last card picked up, and pick up a card yourself. 'This, I think, is the four of diamonds.' This time you pick up the sighted card, the king of clubs, having named the card previously picked up. By this means you have yourself completed the circle and are able to show the cards.

If by any sheer chance a member of your audience taps your sighted card with the pencil, end the trick right away as you will be able to show every card that has been named.

Divination in Pairs
'It is said,' begins the magician, 'that a certain sympathy

exists between pairs of anything. For instance, we all know that twins often choose the same clothes quite independently and even appear to know what each other is thinking. I will now try a little experiment to demonstrate this strange phenomenon.'

So saying, the magician gives two pieces of paper to each of two spectators. Next he or she deals ten pairs of cards face downwards on the table. No one knows the names of the cards. Both spectators are requested to pick up any pair of cards and to write the name of one card upon each of the pieces of paper. This done, the magician picks up the cards still face downwards and proceeds to deal them apparently haphazardly into four rows of five cards each. As the magician says, not knowing the names of the cards because he or she hasn't even seen them, it matters not at all where they are placed.

Now the cards are turned face upwards and the spectators are asked to put each of the folded pieces of paper alongside the row in which the card whose name it bears lies. One spectator places the folded papers to the right of the cards, the other to the left. After pondering for a moment or two, the magician picks up each piece of paper in turn and places it upon a card. When the papers are opened and the names read out, it is found that the magician has placed them accurately upon the chosen pairs.

This is one of the first tricks I learned as a boy. The secret lies in a clever mnemonic consisting of four Latin words: *Mutus, Nomen, Dedit, Cocis*. At first sight, the only strange thing about them would appear to be that they are foreign. A little more thought will reveal that they are formed of twenty letters in four words of five letters each. But more important still they are made up of ten different letters repeated, in other words ten pairs.

Although you apparently throw down the cards haphazardly when making up the four lines of five cards each, and emphasize this in your patter, in reality you are extremely careful to place them in keeping with the mnemonic in the following formation:

$$M\ U\ T\ U\ S$$
$$N\ O\ M\ E\ N$$
$$D\ E\ D\ I\ T$$
$$C\ O\ C\ I\ S$$

You must not only commit these words to memory but also be able to picture them 'in your mind's eye' on the table as shown above. When you place the cards down, you put one card of the first pair at the first position 'M', the first letter of the word MUTUS. The second card of the pair must be placed at the centre of the second row in the other position 'M', the centre letter of the word NOMEN. The third card must go in position 'U', second letter in MUTUS, and the fourth card in position 'U', fourth letter in MUTUS. The next two cards must be placed at 'T' in MUTUS and 'T' in DEDIT. The next at 'S' in MUTUS and 'S' in COCIS, and so on until all twenty cards have been placed.

The following table shows the order in which the cards must be put down to coincide with the mnemonic:

1st row	MUTUS	1	3	5	4	7
2nd row	NOMEN	9	11	2	13	10
3rd row	DEDIT	15	14	16	17	6
4th row	COCIS	19	12	20	18	8

All you need to know in order to 're-pair' the cards is the rows in which they fall. This is revealed when the spectators place their pieces of paper against the rows in which their cards fall.

Thus, if the papers are put against the first and fourth rows, you put the papers on the last cards in the row, the cards dealt seventh and eighth or, in other words, in positions 'S'. If the papers are put against the second and fourth rows, then the paired cards lie second in the second row and second in the fourth row, in positions 'O'.

If both pieces of paper are placed against the same row,

you will need to proceed slightly differently. Although you know which are the paired cards – the two 'U's in MUTUS, the 'N's in NOMEN, the 'D's in DEDIT, and the 'C's in COCIS – you do not know which is which. Instead of picking up each paper and its respective card and showing them one by one, you must pick up both papers and both cards together. Then, you can open one piece of paper, read out the name it bears, and pass this with the correct card for verification. The other paper and card will of course coincide.

It is necessary to practise putting the cards down in the correct sequence quickly whilst apparently throwing them at random. Any hesitation would spoil the illusion.

The idea of having the names of the cards written upon pieces of paper is a nice improvement made by Mr L. Widdop, one of 'The Yellow Perils' authors. It certainly enhances the presentation and at the same time guards against possible forgetfulness on the part of the spectators.

Bringing Back the Ashes

A sheet of paper is torn into eight pieces. Next the magician takes a pack of cards and throws eight of them onto a table. The names of the cards are called out by a spectator and the magician writes them upon the pieces of paper. The papers are folded, dropped into a hat, and one is freely chosen. The remaining pieces are discarded. While the magician's back is turned, the card named on the selected slip is taken from the eight and placed upside down upon the table. The remaining seven cards are removed from sight.

Next the piece of paper bearing the name of the chosen card is burnt and the ashes caught in an ashtray. Then, to the amazement of the audience, the magician rolls up the right sleeve, rubs some of the ashes upon the bare arm, and two black letters appear: KH. That must mean the king of hearts. The chosen card is turned face up and is seen to be indeed the king of hearts.

First you must select the card to be forced. In the foregoing description I used the king of hearts. Make sure that the 'force' card is among the eight thrown onto the table. To ensure that this card is chosen, all you have to do is to write its name on all eight pieces of paper. Of course, your audience think you are writing eight different names so it is necessary to act this out. You might pretend to mishear one of the names, say eight of clubs for the ace of clubs. When one slip of paper has been chosen from the hat, you must remember to remove the evidence by putting the seven remaining slips out of harm's way. From now on it's plain sailing.

A spectator burns the slip of paper and collects the ashes in an ashtray. You rub the ashes on your arm and the initials of the 'force' appear. How? Simple. You write them there beforehand in ordinary soap!

Magical Whist

'You are all whist players, I think,' says the magician. 'And most of you pretty expert at the game, but I will show you how the greatest skill is nullified when opposed to magical or occult knowledge. Here, A! Take the pack into your own hands, shuffle it as much as you like, and take out any four cards. Hand the pack to B, please. Will you do the same, B? Yes! Shuffle the cards to your heart's content and take out any four. Will you take out four cards, C, and you also, D?' The magician hands the pack successively to four spectators in different parts of the room, and permits each to take out and retain four cards.

'Now, just look at your cards, please, and imagine that you are playing whist. Let us suppose that nine tricks have already been disposed of, leaving four still to be played. I want each of you to select mentally the card that you would play, provided it was your turn to lead. You may make your own trumps and you may play to win or throw away, just as you please. Have you selected your respective cards and impressed them firmly on your memories? Good!

Now, from the demonstrations of thought reading that I have already given you, you will recognize that it would be a comparatively easy task for me to look at each set of four cards and name the selected card forthwith, but if I return the cards to the pack without looking at them at all, and mix them thoroughly with the other cards, you will admit that the feat becomes much more difficult.'

Whilst speaking, the magician has been walking round the room, collecting the cards and returning them to the pack before some 'spoil-trick' member of the company has a chance to demand that the cards be named forthwith, which, not being a genuine mindreader, would present the performer with some little difficulty. The magician then returns to the table and shuffles the pack in view of the audience. 'To make the cards more convenient for handling, and also to shuffle them more thoroughly, I will deal them into four whist hands,' declares the magician. The cards are dealt into four heaps, as if dealing for whist, taking care to keep the cards pretty square, one on top of the other (not too obviously orderly, however) so that their sequence is not disturbed.

The magician then takes up one of the heaps, spreads the cards out fanwise, and holds them up to A. 'Is your card in this hand, A? No? Is yours, B? It is? Right! Is yours, C? It is not? Is your card in this group, D? Yes? Good!' The magician closes the fan and looks searchingly at B. 'So you were going to leave it to your partner, B, for I see you would have played the two of clubs. Isn't that so? Now D, you, on the contrary, were out to win for yourself, for you intended to lead off with an ace – the ace of hearts. Am I right, D? B and D admit the assertions and the magician then holds up the second heap fanwise to A. 'Is your card there? No? Is yours amongst them, C? No? Then we can put these aside altogether.' The magician takes up another heap. 'Is your card in this heap, A? It isn't? Is yours, C? Yes? Hum! You were going to see what the queen of spades would bring out, eh? I thought so. Now, A, you seem to be determined to give me a lot of trouble. Is your card in this hand?' The magician holds up the last lot. 'Of course it must be, for it is the only hand left. It is there? Ah! You've been trying to puzzle me all along. You would have led off with an unimportant card – the three of diamonds. Am I right?' A admits that once again the magician is correct.

It is wise to select for the supposed whist players four people in different parts of the room, so that in collecting the sets of cards after the mental selection you have to walk a few paces between each player. Whilst telling the company that you are going to make the feat more difficult by returning the cards to the pack, you collect A's cards and, in turning naturally to walk to B, you slip them to the bottom of the remainder of the pack which you have in your hands.

The pack is held in your left hand, and this hand acts as a cover to conceal the position from the remainder of the company, whilst you naturally turn away from A and interpose your body in that person's view.

Similarly, by the same artifice, you secretly place B's set under A's, C's cards under B's, and D's under C's, so that the sixteen cards that have been in the hands of the players are all at the bottom of the pack. Now the natural assumption on the part of the audience is that the cards returned have been put on top of the pack, and this illusion is of value when you come to shuffle the cards.

This shuffle is a genuine one as far as the top portion of the pack is concerned but fictitious in respect of the bottom part, because it does not disturb the order of the bottom sixteen cards. This false shuffle is an imitation of an orthodox shuffle often used by card players and is performed as follows. Hold the cards in your left hand and push two or three from the top of the pack into the fingers of your right hand. Then push two or three more beneath these. Next, put a few on top, a few beneath, a few on top again, and so on, alternately placing cards beneath and above, until you come to, say, the bottom twenty-four or so (leaving a safe margin). These you push *en bloc* below, thus leaving the sixteen cards at the bottom undisturbed just as they were when collected from the players.

Now deal the cards into four whist hands to 'facilitate handling'. In doing this the first thirty-six cards are of little importance, they merely go to make the first nine cards of each of the four heaps. After these, however, come the sixteen cards from which the mental selections were made, the first or top four being A's, the second four B's, the third C's, and the last or bottom four cards are D's. Continuing the deal then, each of A's four cards becomes the tenth card of one of the hands, B's four become the eleventh cards of the respective heaps, C's the twelfth, and D's the thirteenth and last. The following table illustrates this:

	1st hand 1–9	2nd hand 1–9	3rd hand 1–9	4th hand 1–9	total cards 36
A's cards	10	10	10	10	
B's cards	11	11	11	11	16
C's cards	12	12	12	12	
D's cards	13	13	13	13	

The secret is now disclosed. Whichever 'hand' A indicates as containing the chosen card (and, of course, it may be any one of the heaps), you know that it must be the tenth card in the fan, or, looking at it in a more convenient way, the fourth from the other end. Similarly, you know that B's will be the third from the end, C's the second, and D's the last card in whichever heap is indicated as containing the respective cards. Of course, there may be two or more of the selected cards in the same fan.

Eight Kings

This effect has been used many times on television by well-known magicians. A pack of cards is shuffled and several spectators are asked one by one to take from the pack a small bunch of cards until half of the cards are in the hands of the audience. The magician then takes each member of the audience in turn and names the cards he or she is holding. This is an astounding effect and has helped to make the reputations of several performers.

The secret lies in the use of a 'stacked deck', that is a pack of cards that has been sorted into a special sequence. A clever mnemonic is used to enable you to remember the position of every card in the pack. It sounds an impossible feat but with practice you will find that it becomes second nature to reel off the cards in the correct order. In order to misdirect the audience into thinking that the cards are completely haphazard in the pack, you must execute a false shuffle, details of which appear on pages 28 to 30.

Fan the cards face downwards before the first helper and allow, say, five or six cards to be taken from the pack near to the top. Make sure that the next spectator takes his or her bunch of cards commencing with the one immediately below those previously taken. The next likewise, and so on. In this way, although the cards are taken from the middle of the pack, they do run in sequence from the first card in the first spectator's bunch to the last card in the last spectator's bunch. And you need only know the first spectator's first card to be able to work out all the other chosen cards. To do this, all you need is a glimpse at the card lying above the first card chosen, in other words, the bottom card of the top portion of the pack left in your hand when the bunches of cards have been removed.

Now for the mnemonic which I think will make everything clear. You will need to learn by heart the following sentence:

Eight kings threatened to send nine fine ladies for one sick knave.

That shouldn't be too difficult, should it? I first learnt it when I was about six years old and it's stayed in my memory ever since. But what does it mean? This breakdown will help:

Eight kings threa-tened to send nine fine ladies for one
  8   king   3   10   2   7   9   5 queen 4 ace
sick knave.
  6   jack

It will be also necessary to learn the following sequence: clubs, hearts, spades, diamonds. And there is even a mnemonic to help you with that: CHaSeD. Remember CHaSeD and you will always know the correct sequence for the suits.

Before the performance you must sort the cards into the special order, or in magician's language 'stack the deck'. The pack thus arranged, reading from the top card, should appear as shown in Figure 46.

The cards may be cut without disturbing the sequence, but the only shuffles allowed are false ones. Now that you know the secret order of the cards, let's see how it works in practice. Say the first spectator takes a bunch of cards right out of the middle of the pack and they are the nine of diamonds, five of clubs, queen of hearts, four of spades, and ace of diamonds. The next spectator's bunch must start with the six of clubs, the jack of hearts, and so on. The rest of the bunches must also follow in sequence. Eventually you will be left with two portions of cards, the top and bottom parts of the pack. Put them together by placing the top portion under the bottom portion.

The new bottom card of the pack will be the seven of spades, the card originally above the nine of diamonds (the first card of the first bunch). Once you know the name of this key card, you are able to work out the names of all the selected cards. You go to each member of the audience in turn, silently count how many cards he or she is holding, and name that number of cards in accordance with the sequence. Your audience will give you credit for second-sight or at least X-ray eyes.

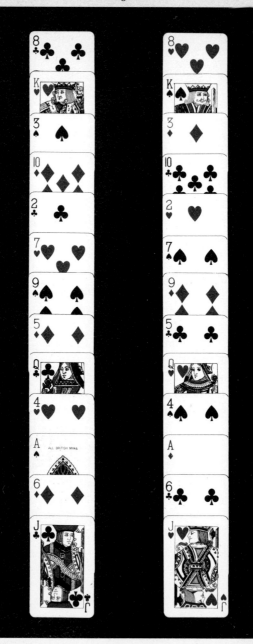

Fig. 46

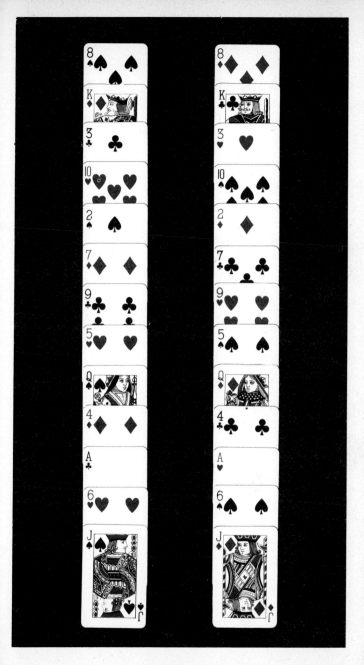

Master Card Tricks
The Diminishing Cards

The magician shows several normal-sized playing cards in a fan. Closing the fan, the magician gives them a squeeze and they become smaller. Another squeeze and they become smaller still. Once more a squeeze and they are even smaller. Eventually they become so very small that they disappear altogether.

Only three different-sized sets of similar cards are required. Set 1 consists of five normal-sized cards. Set 2 consists of five cards of the same denominations and suits as the normal cards but half their size. Set 3 also duplicates the five cards but these are a quarter of normal size.

Hold the three sets of cards altogether in your left hand with Set 3 against your fingers, Set 2 next, and Set 1 last, held by your thumb (Fig. 47) and fanned in full view (Fig. 48). Close the Set 1 fan of cards with your right hand, pushing them lower down into your left hand. Fan them out again and they will appear smaller (Fig. 49). Push the cards together again with your right hand but this time palm them off (Fig. 50), at the same time pulling Set 2 into view with your right fingers (Fig. 51) and fanning them out (Fig. 52).

Pick up a normal-sized card from your table or pocket,

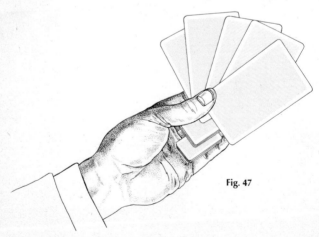

Fig. 47

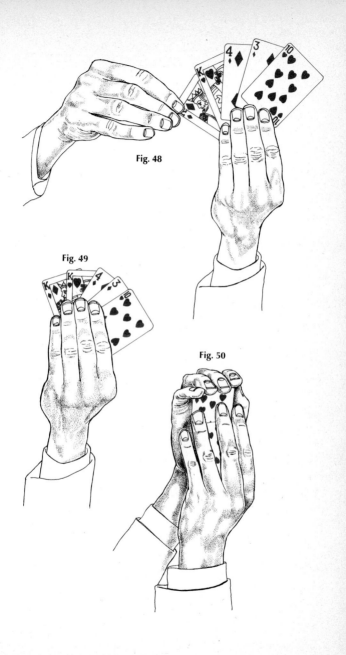

Fig. 48

Fig. 49

Fig. 50

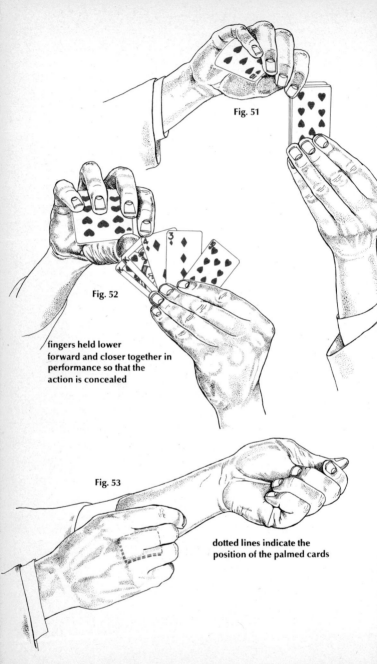

Fig. 51

Fig. 52

fingers held lower
forward and closer together in
performance so that the
action is concealed

Fig. 53

dotted lines indicate the
position of the palmed cards

at the same time 'ditching' or secretly disposing of Set 1. Demonstrate how small the cards have become by comparing them with the normal-sized card. Lay it down on your table.

For the next diminish, close the Set 2 fan, push the cards lower into your left hand and fan them out again. Then close the fan once more, palming the cards off in your right hand and bringing Set 3 into view at your fingertips. Ditch Set 2 as you pick up another normal card for a final comparison. Diminish the cards yet again by closing the Set 3 fan, pushing them lower in your hand, and re-fanning. Finally squeeze them in your right hand and palm them off as you appear to place them in the left (Fig. 53).

Pick up a normal card, at the same time ditching Set 3. Hold the card horizontally in your right hand and appear to place the infinitesimal cards upon it with your left hand. Blow gently on the 'cards' and they have completely disappeared!

The Famous Card Stab

For this trick the magician is first blindfolded with a handkerchief. A card is selected and returned to the pack. The pack is then cut into several heaps, and the heaps mixed up so that all the cards in the pack lie haphazardly face downwards on the table. Now the magician, still blindfolded, takes a knife and plunges it into one card. The knife is raised and there, stuck on the point, face towards the audience, is the chosen card.

Fold the handkerchief into a bandage and hold its centre against your forehead. Ask someone to tie the ends at the back of your head. As this is done, appear to adjust the handkerchief so that it completely obscures your vision. In reality position it so that, although it is placed fairly over your eyes, you are still able to see downwards at either side of your nose.

Ask a spectator to take any card from the pack and hand the depleted pack to you. Of course you must act the whole time as though you can't see a thing. Cut the pack for the return of the card, make a break above it with your little finger as you close the pack, and perform the two-handed pass to bring the chosen card to the top of the pack.

Cut the cards into four or five heaps on the table. Then scatter each heap in turn all over the table top, keeping an eye on the whereabouts of the chosen card. Ask for the knife to be handed to you and encircle the cards two or three times. Then suddenly bring it down and spear the chosen card.

The Thirty-Card Trick

One of the most often performed card tricks is known by many different names. I call it 'The Thirty-Card Trick'. The magician asks two gentlemen members of the audience for assistance. Next he or she shows an ordinary pack of cards and asks one of the helpers to count out thirty cards. To emphasize the number, the second helper is asked to count them again. One of them now cuts the cards, at random, into two heaps. Both helpers are asked to empty their inside coat-pockets and one of them selects a heap, puts it in his inside pocket, and buttons up his coat. The remaining heap is counted by the second helper and placed by him in his inside coat-pocket. The magician declares the intention of making five cards pass, one at a time, from one gentleman's pocket to the other. On removing and counting the cards, it is found that five have left one heap and joined the other.

After the thirty cards have been counted a second time, take them and square them up between both hands before passing them back to the first helper. In so doing, palm off five cards in your right hand. Have the cards cut and ask one helper to choose a heap – it does not matter which. Get him to put this heap into his pocket and button his coat.

Ask the second helper to count how many cards he has in his heap; say it is nine. You then state that, as there are nine cards in the remaining heap, there must be twenty-one cards in the first helper's pocket. Motion towards the nine cards on the table, with your right hand scarcely brushing them in the direction of the second helper, while requesting that he take the nine cards and put them in his empty inside pocket. Undercover of this move, add the five palmed cards. When the cards are finally removed from the pockets and counted, five cards will have left the twenty-one cards so that only sixteen remain, and five cards will have joined the nine cards, making fourteen. Another miracle has been performed!

The Rising Cards

Possibly the greatest of all card tricks, 'The Rising Cards' can be performed using many different methods. First I give the standard method as performed by most amateur magicians. Next a method recommended by David Devant as being simple to perform yet extremely effective. And lastly two versions of the great American illusionist Howard Thurston's method, with which he made his reputation. I had the very great pleasure of seeing Thurston's successor, Dante, perform this trick at the Garrick Theatre in London many years ago.

The basic effect is the same in each case. Three cards are selected by members of the audience and returned to the pack. The pack is isolated in a glass tumbler or simply held by the performer. One by one the cards rise up out of the pack at the magician's command.

The Standard Rising Cards   To perform the standard effect you have to prepare a special set-up as follows. Take eight playing cards and glue them together in pairs for added strength. Make a hole in the centre a little way from the top of each pair of cards. Tie a large knot at one end of a length of black thread and then thread all four sets of cards on to it. Attach a safety pin to the free end. Push the three cards that are to rise down between the double cards so that they rest

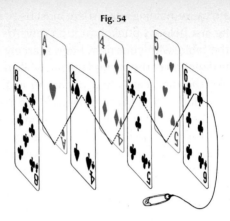

on the thread (Fig. 54). Thus, if the thread is pulled, the duplicate cards will be made to rise one at a time until almost clear of the 'pack'.

To perform, have the set-up lying face upwards on your table, hidden behind a silk or some piece of apparatus. The loose end of the thread should be pinned to the table cloth, which must in turn be securely anchored to the table with drawing pins. You will also need a glass tumbler and an ordinary pack of cards.

First force the three cards, duplicates of which lie in the set-up, on three members of the audience and have them returned at random. Place the pack face up on the table, secretly on top of the set-up. Take up the tumbler and show it to be without preparation. Pick up the pack again, but this time with the addition of the set-up at the rear, and place it in the tumbler. With the tumbler in your right hand, carry it forward until the thread is taut. Now, by moving the glass slowly forward, the cards will rise one at a time.

The Elastic Rising Cards   Method number two makes use of a 'gimmick' or unseen piece of apparatus originally designed to cause a card to jump clear out of the pack. It consists of four cards glued together in pairs with a short piece of elastic fixed between them. Three of these gimmicks are required, together with two packs of cards.

Take the three cards which are to rise and place one of them in each of the gimmicks. Put all three gimmicks at the centre of one pack, and push down the 'chosen' cards against the elastics until they lie flush with the rest of the pack. Secure the cards with two elastic bands, one around the length and one around the width of the cards. Place this prepared pack in an easily accessible position, either in a waistcoat (vest) pocket or tucked in a cummerbund or belt.

Force the three cards, duplicates of which lie in the gimmicks, from the ordinary pack and have them returned. Explain that you will secure the cards with elastic bands in both directions so that the three cards, wherever they are in the pack, cannot be tampered with. As you return to the table, 'switch' or secretly exchange the ordinary pack for the prepared pack.

State that you will cause the cards to rise but must first remove the lengthwise elastic band to enable them to do so. Remove the band but immediately place your left forefinger on top of the pack to stop the cards from rising prematurely. All you have to do is very gently release pressure on the pack and draw back your left forefinger to allow the cards to rise one at a time.

The Thurston Rising Cards   For this famous version you will need a special piece of apparatus called a 'reel', stocked by many magic-dealers. This consists of a small, round metal box which contains a drum that works on a clock spring. Around the drum is wound a length of black thread. When the thread is pulled and released, it is drawn back into the reel as the drum turns. On one side of the reel is fastened a safety pin with which to fix it to your clothing. On the other side is a button which, when pressed, releases the thread to be drawn back into the reel. Fix the reel at your waist on the left-hand side under your coat

(Fig. 55). At the end of the thread fix a small dab of wax and attach this to a waistcoat (vest) button or some similarly accessible place.

Have any three cards chosen and pass them to the top of the pack. As you return to the table, detach the wax from its button and press it against the top card of the pack, one of the chosen cards. Hold the pack in your left hand, bringing your left elbow over the button on the reel. Pass your right hand around the pack to show that no threads or wires are attached. As your right hand passes underneath the cards it encounters the thread, which you must allow to come between your first and second fingers. Draw the thread up with your right hand until you are holding your hand level with your head.

Without moving your right hand even a fraction, press against the reel button with your left elbow. This will release the thread, which is drawn inside the reel and causes the back card, one of the chosen three, to rise not only clear of the pack but right up through the air until it reaches your right hand (Fig. 56). Release pressure on the reel, place the card on the face of the pack, and secretly remove the wax.

Affix the wax to the back card, put pressure on the button of the reel once more, and wave your right hand around the pack. Again secure the thread between your

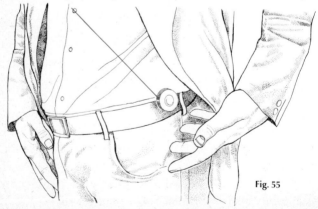

Fig. 55

68

Fig. 56

first and second fingers and draw it out of the reel until your right hand has reached the same position as before. You are now ready to 'rise' the second of the chosen cards. Repeat the above moves to rise the third card.

This is a very difficult trick to perform, even for an experienced magician. You must achieve strong misdirection to cover the various moves. This can be done by pacing to and from the audience, asking for the names of the chosen cards to be called on each occasion. It is of course more suited to platform or stage performance as close up the thread will undoubtedly be seen. Under stage conditions, however, the following version is by far the best.

The stage version of the Thurston Rising Cards   The effect of this version is very similar to that in the previous method but, instead of the reel, a much simpler device is used for motive power.

A black thread is stretched across the stage at just above your head height. The thread passes over small pulleys, or

through small hooks, fixed at either side of the stage in the wings with about 4 feet (122 cm) hanging down in each case. Attached to each end of the thread are about twelve cards which act as counterweights. These keep the thread taut but enable the performer to pull down the centre of the thread and attach it to a card which, when released, is drawn up in the air by their weight. In addition to this set-up, you will need duplicates of the cards to be chosen and these must be fitted with tiny clips or hooks at the back.

Force the three 'chosen' cards but, on returning to the stage, add the prepared cards to the back of the pack. Stand centre stage with the pack in your left hand and pass your right hand around and over it to 'prove' that there are no threads or wires. As your hand passes well over the pack, secretly secure the thread and bring it down behind the pack, hooking the hindermost card onto it. Hold this card to the pack with your left thumb. To cause the card to rise, simply remove your left thumb and it will float gracefully up into your right hand. Repeat with the other two cards.

Catching coins from the air, or The Miser's Dream, made famous by T. Nelson Downs

COIN MAGIC

Sleight of Hand with Coins
The basic palm

To be able to palm a coin in what is known as the 'palm proper' is an essential skill for the coin conjurer. As with most sleights, it will be difficult at first, but the more you practise the easier it will become, until you can perform the move completely subconsciously. This is the eventual aim with all sleights and indeed with the working of all your tricks. Ideally the performer should be equally adept using either the right or the left hand so practise with both.

First hold the coin between your forefinger and thumb for all to see (Fig. 1). Slide it with your thumb onto the second and third fingers, withdrawing the forefinger. This leaves the coin held for an instant between your second and third fingers and your thumb (Fig. 2).

You now remove your thumb and press the coin into your palm. The coin is held in this position by a slight inward movement of the muscles of the fleshy part of the ball of the thumb, which grips the coin against the other fleshy part of your palm below the little finger (Fig. 3). You can now open your second and third fingers, leaving the coin safely held in the palm. With the back of your hand towards the audience you can move your fingers about quite naturally without dislodging the hidden coin. As far as your audience is concerned the hand is empty.

With practice you will find it possible to pick up a glass tumbler with the tips of your finges while holding a coin in the palm proper. You will also be able to palm several coins one on top of the other. In this chapter you will find a great many uses for this most important sleight.

The finger palm

Another basic sleight you will need to learn is the 'finger palm'. Despite its name, the palm is not actually involved as the coin is simply hidden by the top joints of your two middle fingers.

Fig. 1

Fig. 2

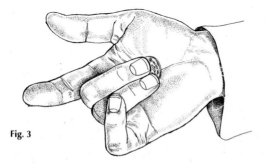

Fig. 3

75

As with the palm proper, you start with the coin held between your first finger and thumb (Fig. 1). Then slide the coin down until its top edge is resting against the first joints of your two middle fingers (Fig. 4). Immediately withdraw your forefinger and thumb and at the same time bend your two middle fingers in slightly so that the coin is securely trapped between the first and second joints (Fig. 5).

With this palm, your fingers are restricted but it is possible, with care, to show your hand to be 'empty' on both sides.

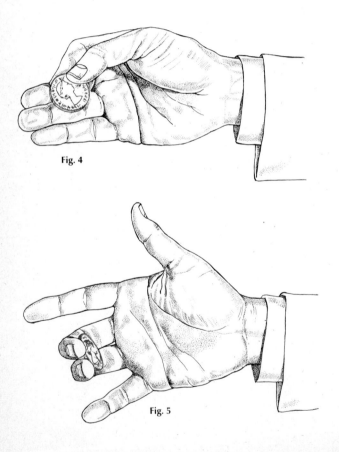

Fig. 4

Fig. 5

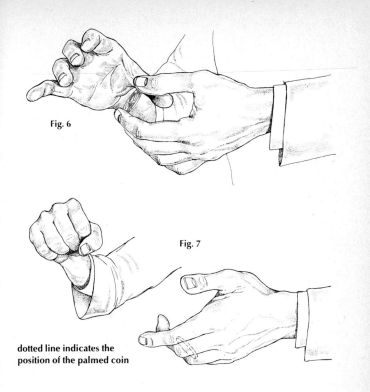

Fig. 6

Fig. 7

dotted line indicates the
position of the palmed coin

The French Drop

This is probably the most used and abused sleight in the
magician's repertoire. You appear to take the coin from
one hand into the other but in reality leave it behind in the
first hand.

The Downs version   T. Nelson Downs, the greatest coin
conjurer of his day, performed it as follows. The coin is held
between the first and second fingers and thumb of your
left hand. You move this hand up as though to put the coin
into your right hand, which appears to take it (Fig. 6). But,
as you begin to close your right fingers to grasp the coin,
allow it to slip down past your thumb into your left palm.
Complete the closing of your right hand and move it away
as though containing the coin (Fig. 7). It is really essential

that you follow your right hand with your eyes to mis-direct your audience's attention to it and to enable you to drop your left hand casually to your side, transferring the hidden coin to the palm proper if desired.

The author's version   As with all magic, the devotee will find his own variations on sleights and I have found this version of the 'French Drop' works very successfully for me.

I hold the coin in my right hand between the two middle fingers and thumb but, instead of my fingers pointing upwards as in the Downs method, they point towards the audience, revealing the full surface of the coin (Fig. 8). I then bring up my left hand, its back towards the audience, and appear to take the coin, fingers at the front, thumb at the rear. By fractionally raising my right thumb under cover of the left hand, the coin is allowed to drop backwards flat onto my right fingers, ready for the finger palm. Meanwhile the left hand closes as though containing the coin and moves away to the left followed by my eyes. To further emphasize the supposed whereabouts of the coin, I point at the left hand with my right forefinger for a second or two before casually dropping this hand to my side.

Fig. 8

The De Manche Change

It is often necessary to change one coin for another and this is one of the best methods. It is an improvement on other sleights as only one hand is required and it is impossible for the coins to clink against each other. In conjurer's parlance, this is called 'talking'. Although it has been suggested that this method can be used for a visible change from, say, a bronze to a silver coin, I would not recommend it. Much better to use it secretly to substitute one coin for a similar coin. If it is necessary to switch a marked coin for a duplicate, the 'De Manche Change' is ideal.

The sleight can be performed with the back of your hand either towards your audience or away from it. The position of your hand and the timing of the move are entirely dependent upon the situation created by the trick you are performing. As it requires only one hand, sufficient misdirection can easily be achieved by picking up something with the free hand at the right moment.

One coin (Coin A) is held between the tips of your forefinger and thumb, while the other (Coin B) is hidden behind the remaining three fingers, which are bent into your palm (Fig. 9). Press Coin A with your thumb onto the second finger and at the same time move your forefinger to the edge of the coin (Fig. 10).

Now, using your forefinger, slide Coin A to the base of your thumb and grip it between this and the first phalange (Fig. 11). Next extend your second, third, and little fingers, release their grip on Coin B, and at the same time move your thumb until its tip rests upon the coin (Fig. 12).

You then push Coin B with the ball of your thumb to the tip of your forefinger and hold it there. In doing this, you will automatically release Coin A, which turns over onto its edge and slides into the place behind your slightly bent second, third, and little fingers just vacated by Coin B (Fig. 13). This completes the change and the trick continues as though nothing has happened.

With practice these movements will become completely

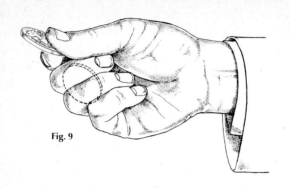

Fig. 9

Fig. 10

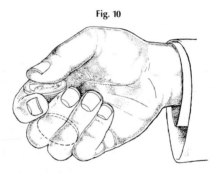

dotted line indicates the position of the palmed coin

Fig. 11

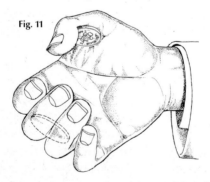

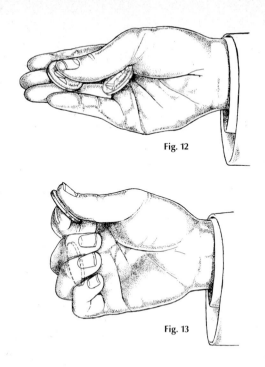

Fig. 12

Fig. 13

automatic so that you can perform the sleight subconsciously while concentrating your attention on some other matter, thus completely misdirecting your audience. This is the quintessence of good magic.

The back and front palm

That great American coin conjurer, T. Nelson Downs, had a most elaborate method of performing this sleight. No doubt it was suitable for the audiences of his day, when acts moved along at a very leisurely pace compared with the lively, high-speed entertainments of today. However, the sleight has a useful part to play in the performance of the most famous of coin tricks, 'The Miser's Dream', so here is a streamlined version.

The magician shows a coin and apparently throws it into the air, where it promptly disappears. Then the hand is shown, back and front, to the audience, proving that the coin is not concealed there. This move can be repeated a couple of times and then the coin can be recovered where and when the performer wishes.

Bring the coin to a position resting upon your second and third fingers but gripped between your fore and little fingers (Fig. 14). Next draw down your two middle fingers until the tips rest behind the coin at the side nearest the palm. If you now straighten these fingers and exert a slight pressure on the edge of the coin (Fig. 15), it will revolve between your fore and little fingers and come to a position flat against the back of your hand, still held by your fore and little fingers and hidden by the middle fingers (Fig. 16).

The sleight should be performed very quickly, covered by a short movement of your hand as though you are throwing the coin away. To make the coin reappear at this point, you simply reverse the foregoing moves. However, the complete action enables you to turn your hand round and show the back of the hand also empty.

To do this, you first release hold of the coin with your little finger so that it is held edgeways between your fore and second fingers (Fig. 17). Next bend your fingers round towards your palm and, with the help of your second and third fingers, transfer the coin to your palm (Fig. 18). At the same time, turn your hand at the wrist, bring the back of your hand towards the audience, and extend your thumb and fingers.

A complete reversal of this move – i.e. picking up the coin with your two middle fingers and replacing it between your first and second fingers – enables you to show the front of your hand.

Back and front palming, whether it be with a coin or a playing card, is one of the most difficult sleights to learn. Practise in front of a mirror over and over again and do not attempt to perform it in public until you have mastered it.

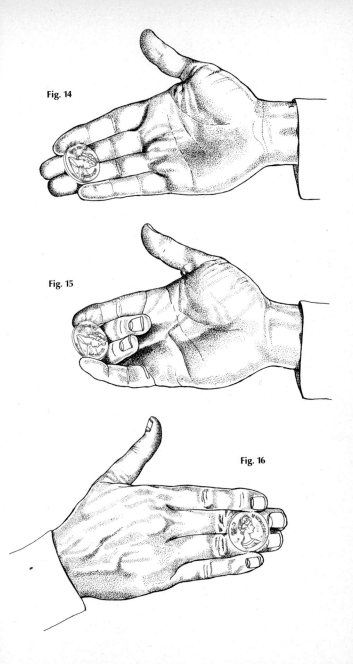

Fig. 14

Fig. 15

Fig. 16

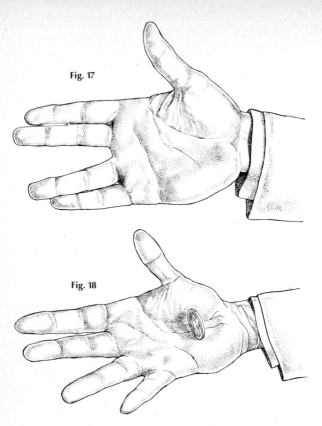

Fig. 17

Fig. 18

Coin Magic without Apparatus
A simple coin vanish

A coin is placed down on a table for all to see. It is picked up in the right hand and transferred to the left, from whence it completely disappears. The coin may be reproduced from the pocket of a spectator or elsewhere at the performer's discretion.

It is best to do this trick seated at a table. Place the coin before you, about 2 inches (5·08 cm) from the table's edge. Then cover it with the fingers of your right hand and draw the coin quickly towards you, closing the hand as it leaves the table. But, instead of picking up the coin, give it a sharp blow with the tips of your fingers and shoot it straight up your sleeve.

Now pretend to put the coin into your left hand and close it. Make a squeezing motion as if rubbing the coin away and at the same time slowly drop your right hand to your side and recover the coin, which will drop into your hand from your sleeve. Slowly open your left hand and show that the coin has vanished. You are now able to reproduce it from a spectator's pocket, or your own, or any other suitable place at will. This trick is greatly enhanced if you first have the coin marked by a spectator.

Another simple vanish

For this simple method of vanishing a coin you will not need a table. A coin is spun in the air, caught in the right hand, and immediately placed in the left hand, from which it disappears.

Spin the coin up in the air in the usual way but, as you appear to catch it, let it fall behind your hand, which you instantly close, and straight down your sleeve. If you position yourself with your right side towards the audience, the passage of the coin down your sleeve will go undetected. Always check your sleeve beforehand to make sure it is well open. As in the previous trick, pretend to place the coin in your left hand and conclude in a similar manner.

Heads or Tails

A coin is spun upon the floor or a table and, even though the performer is blindfolded, he or she can tell whether it falls heads or tails.

To do this, you will need to prepare a coin by cutting a notch in its edge so that a tiny point projects from it. The notch must not be perceptible to the eye, but enough to make a distinct difference in the manner the coin runs down when it has been spun.

Borrow a coin and, as you are being blindfolded with a suitable scarf, secretly switch it, using the 'De Manche

Change', for the prepared coin. Once blindfold, you spin the coin upwards into the air and allow it to fall onto the floor or table. If it falls notched side upwards, it will run down with a long, continuous whirring sound, a sound that becomes fainter and fainter until it ceases altogether. If it falls notch side downwards, however, it will spin itself out much quicker and settle down with a sudden flop. The difference in sound will not be sufficient to give the game away to your audience but, with practice, it will be easily discernible to you.

You must conceal the fact that it is the sound that gives you the clue you need. Far better to suggest that you have X-ray eyes and can 'see' through the scarf or that you are able to read the minds of your audience.

The Mesmerized Coin

The performer balances a coin on its edge at the tips of extended fingers. After making a few mysterious passes over it, the coin slowly sinks backwards until it lies flat.

Although this trick does not require special apparatus, you do need something extra – an ordinary pin. Place the pin upon a bright silver coin. Pick up both coin and pin with the forefinger and thumb of your left hand, your thumb covering the point of the pin. Casually show back and front in a sweeping motion so that the audience do not get too good a look. As far as the spectators are concerned, you are simply showing a silver coin.

Slide the pin across the coin with your thumb until the head protrudes about $\frac{1}{2}$ inch (1·27 cm) over the edge. At the same time extend the fingers of your right hand, palm uppermost, and place the coin edge-down across your first and second fingers. The head of the pin should be gripped tightly between these two fingers. In this way the coin can be made to stand almost vertically (Fig. 19).

By slightly relaxing the pressure of your fingers, you can cause the coin to tilt slowly backwards until it rests flat on your fingers. The pin will now be completely hidden between

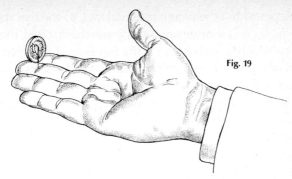

Fig. 19

your fingers so the coin can be tossed into the air with your right hand, caught in the left, and passed out for examination. As already pointed out, this trick is best performed with a bright new coin so that the pin is less noticeable.

The Coin Fold

This is one of the classic coin effects. If performed well, it is extremely convincing. The version described here is exactly as it was performed by that great English magician Charles Bertram.

A coin is placed in a piece of paper and folded in at all sides. The performer immediately tears up the paper, and the coin has vanished.

You will require a piece of paper, newspaper will do, about 4 inches × 6 inches (10·16 cm × 15·24 cm) and a fairly large coin. Before the presentation, make a crease across the paper so that, when folded, one side of the paper is about 1 inch (2·54 cm) shorter than the other.

You show the piece of paper in your left hand, fold it at the crease, and place the coin between the two sides of the paper. Keep your left thumb and fingers upon the coin and pull the sides of the paper together, the shorter half of the paper being away from the audience (Fig. 20). Then double the sides in (Fig. 21).

You should now be holding the packet with one hand at each side so that you can easily bend over the top of it with your forefingers (Fig. 22). This apparently completely seals the coin within the paper. In actual fact, as the rear half of the paper was shorter when you made the first fold, the top piece which is folded over is the top only of the front half and not both halves, and the packet which seems so fairly made is really open all along the top.

Now with the packet in your right hand, tap it against a table, or chair back, to prove that the coin is still there. Next take the packet with your left hand at the bottom edge, turning it upside down. This allows the coin to slide out into your right hand, straight into the finger palm (Fig. 23).

Hold the packet in your left hand at shoulder height, looking at it mysteriously for an instant. Then tear it slowly into tiny pieces, showing the coin has completely disappeared. The coin may either simply be ditched at your convenience or produced from someone's pocket or from some piece of apparatus.

My own version of this effect varies little from the Charles Bertram routine. But the end is greatly improved if, having torn the paper into tiny pieces, the performer can show both hands unmistakably empty. After all, if the coin is no longer in the paper, the audience are led to only one conclusion – it must be hidden in the hands.

If I may refer you back to the original routine: at one stage the left hand takes the packet from the right, leaving

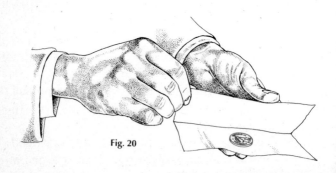

Fig. 20

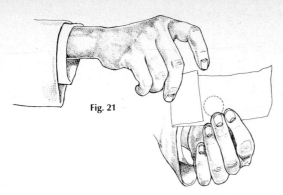

Fig. 21

dotted line indicates the position of the coin

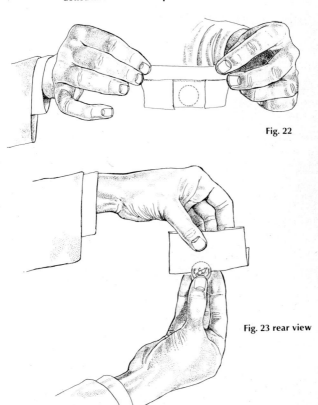

Fig. 22

Fig. 23 rear view

the coin behind in the finger palm; the packet is then held at shoulder height. It is at this point that I get rid of the coin.

The method I use depends entirely upon the situation at the time. If I am performing under bar conditions with the audience close around me, it is a simple matter to slip the coin into my right-hand jacket pocket. In similar conditions, it is also often possible to ditch the coin altogether onto the floor. Under more formal conditions, I can sometimes lose the coin on my table behind some piece of apparatus or a handkerchief. Whichever method you use, it will leave both hands free to tear up the paper and show that the coin has completely vanished.

The Chinese Coin Trick

This trick was invented by the great Chung Ling Soo. The magician borrows a large handkerchief, spreads it flat on a table, and places a borrowed coin in the centre. The four corners of the handkerchief are now gathered together and a borrowed finger-ring is slipped over them and pushed down until it is close to the coin. The magician once more places the handkerchief flat on the table with the coin, trapped by the ring, underneath. Two members of the audience are now asked to hold down the handkerchief by placing their forefingers on two of the four corners. Another handkerchief is borrowed and laid over the first one so as to cover the centre, where the ring and coin are, but leave the corners still held down free. It seems impossible that under these conditions the magician can remove the coin and ring but that is exactly what he or she proposes to do. Placing both hands under the upper handkerchief, both the coin and ring are brought forth in seconds.

The secret is very simple. You have to make sure that the two corners of the lower handkerchief nearer to you are not spread out to their fullest extent, but are a few inches (or cms) closer together than the opposite ends. This will not be noticed although it allows a little fullness in the handkerchief on your side.

Then, all you have to do, under the cover of the second handkerchief, is gather up the fullness of the lower one, making sure that you do not give it a tell-tale tug. When you have worked the fullness right up to the ring, the folds must be pushed down through it until there is a large enough hole to enable you to release the coin (Fig. 24).

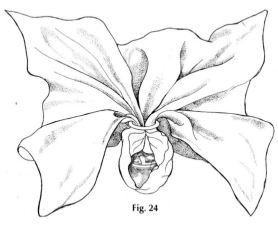

Fig. 24

Once the coin has been removed, the ring will also be free. Be sure to straighten out the lower handkerchief before allowing the top one to be removed, and you will have presented your audience with a really baffling mystery.

The Chinese Coin and String Trick

A Chinese coin with a hole in the centre is threaded upon a string, and the two ends of the string are held by a spectator. Next a handkerchief is thrown over the coin and, under its cover, the magician removes the coin, although the ends of the string are securely held throughout.

To perform this trick you will require two perforated coins. These must be similar in appearance and bear the same date. Failing real coins, a pair of large washers will serve.

Conceal one coin in your right hand in the palm proper. Hand out the string and duplicate coin for examination so that the spectators can satisfy themselves there is no

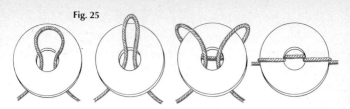
Fig. 25

deception. Ask a spectator to thread the coin on the string and to hold the two ends out in front of him or her. Make sure that the string is not pulled taut but allowed to sag a little.

You now borrow a small handkerchief and drape it over the coin. This is, of course, being used to cover your manipulations, so make the standard excuse that 'spirits work better in the dark'. With both hands under the handkerchief, you must slide the suspended coin to the left and proceed to loop the string through the duplicate coin that was palmed in your right hand. To do this, make a tiny loop at the centre of the string and press it up through the hole in the coin. Next, pass the loop over the top of the coin and right down the back (Fig. 25). The assistant from the audience is then asked to pull the string a little tighter. This ensures that the coin is securely held on the string.

You now have secretly to remove the first coin, which is still suspended on the string. To do this, you ask again for the string to be pulled tighter and slide both hands apart towards each end of the string to show what you mean. The original coin is slid along too, under cover of your left hand. Pretend to show a little impatience. Say, 'Tighter, tighter', and take the string out of the assistant's hands to emphasize what you mean. Then, hand it back again but with your hands at the extreme ends so that the assistant is forced to take the string inside your hands. This enables you to slide off the extra coin and pocket it without being spotted.

Here comes a subtle move. You take off the handkerchief, saying 'Let's see how we are getting on.' Everyone can now see that the coin is still on the string, but apparently more firmly held than before. Cover it once more with the handkerchief and, with a simple movement, free the coin from the string and allow everything to be examined. To release the coin, simply slide the loop back over the top of the coin and it can be pulled clear.

The Coin through the Table Trick

Here is an easy little trick which is done with the performer seated behind a table. Two coins are borrowed and marked. They are placed near the edge of the table in front of the performer. One coin is picked up in the left hand and taken underneath the table. The other coin is picked up in the right hand and held above the table. Suddenly the performer slaps the right hand down on the table and a coin is heard to join the one already in the left hand. Removing the right hand, the performer shows the coin has gone and, on opening the left hand, the two borrowed and marked coins are revealed.

The first coin is indeed picked up quite normally in your left hand and held underneath the table. However, on seeming to pick up the other one in your right hand, you actually slide it off the table onto your lap, closing your hand at the same time as though it contains the coin. Immediately the coin lands on your lap, pick it up in your left hand, making sure that it does not 'talk' against the coin already held. All you have to do now to complete the trick is slap your empty right hand down on the table, allow the two coins in your left hand to clink together, and then bring this hand out and display the two coins.

The Coin in an Orange Trick

Two oranges are shown to the audience and someone is invited to choose one of them. The other orange is cut up to show that it is without trickery. A table knife is pushed into the chosen orange, which is given to the helper to hold. A coin is borrowed and marked for later identification.

94

The coin disappears, but when the orange is cut open, the coin is discovered inside.

You need a duplicate coin which you mark by scratching a cross on it, using a penknife. Slit one of the oranges and insert the coin. Now, begin by showing the oranges and have one selected. If the prepared orange is chosen, you just proceed with the trick. If the ordinary orange is chosen, you cut it up, pass the pieces out for examination, and use the other orange for the trick. This is known as 'conjurer's choice'. Push the table knife into the slit already made in the 'chosen' orange and give it to someone to hold. By using the same slit, you destroy the evidence.

Borrow a coin and have it marked with a penknife, but make sure that the person holding the orange on the knife does not see the mark – you can't be certain that it will be a cross. Vanish the coin by whichever method you prefer as long as it leaves the coin in your possession. The rattle box would be very suitable (see page 116). Have the orange cut open to reveal your marked coin. Then, as you go to return it to its 'owner', switch it for the real borrowed coin.

The Change-Over Coins

Two contrasting coins are borrowed, the owners being requested to mark them. Each coin is placed in a borrowed pocket handkerchief and, although the handkerchiefs are held by members of the audience, the coins change places.

In addition to the borrowed coins (Coins A1 and B1) and handkerchiefs, you need one duplicate coin (Coin A). While Coins A1 and B1 are being marked, you palm Coin A in your left hand. You receive the marked coins in your right hand and appear to transfer them to the left. In fact, you transfer only Coin B1, retaining Coin A1 in your right hand. The audience sees the two contrasting coins (B1 and A) in your left hand and imagines that they are the marked coins. You place these two openly on the table.

Then, with your right hand, pick up Coin B1, casually drawing attention to the mark. Throw a handkerchief over this hand, and under its cover switch Coin B1 for Coin A1, which you have palmed. The 'De Manche Change' is ideal for this. Hand the handkerchief showing the shape of Coin A1 inside it to a spectator with the request that he or she grips the handkerchief just below the coin. The audience thinks that this is Coin B1.

You now take Coin A, which the audience thinks is the marked Coin A1, and cover it with the second handkerchief, at the same time switching it for Coin B1. You request another member of your audience to hold this handkerchief as before. Dispose of the palmed Coin A. After the usual mystic waves of the hands, ask the spectators to check the coins and they are seen to have changed places.

Invisible Flight

As a boy this was one of my favourite tricks. The performer borrows four small coins, places one in each palm, and, having closed the hands into fists with palms uppermost, asks a member of the audience to place the other two coins upon the fingernails of each hand. The performer tosses the visible coins into the air apparently with the intention of catching them, misses in fact, and asks that they be replaced. The next attempt is successful and the coins are caught one in each hand. The performer then says that one coin will be made to leave the right hand and join the two coins in the left. A magic word is uttered and both hands opened, whereupon it is seen that the left hand contains three coins and the right only one. One coin must have passed invisibly between the two hands.

As described above, you borrow four coins, hold one in each hand, and balance one on top of the fingernails of each hand. Saying that you will throw the balancing coins upwards and catch them, you appear to try but miss. In fact, as your hands move upwards to make the throw, you open your left-hand fingers, secure the coin that is lying on top of the fingers, and quickly close them again. At the same time, both coins are allowed to drop from your right hand as though they are the coins that were exposed, one from each hand. Keep your hands closed and the audience will imagine that there is still a coin in each.

Ask for the coins to be replaced on the fingernails of each hand, and make the throw again. This time, however, you simply open your hands under cover of the throwing movement and allow a coin to fall into each hand. This means that one hand contains three coins and the other only one. Open your hands to show that such is the case and the trick is complete.

The Coin through the Hand Trick

The magician takes a borrowed penny in one hand and rubs it to and fro across the back of the other hand. The coin apparently passes right through the hand and is discovered in its palm.

To perform, borrow a coin and hold it between the tips of your right-hand thumb and forefinger. Rub the coin on the back of your closed left hand (Fig. 26). Suddenly stop and say you are sorry but you should have shown your left hand empty first. Keep your right hand in the same position but open your left hand and hold it out obviously empty.

Now comes the important bit. As you turn your left hand over and form it into a fist once more, drop the coin from

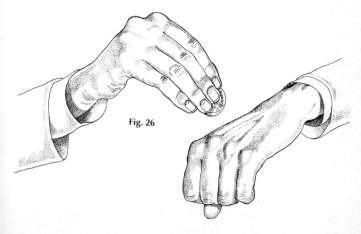

Fig. 26

97

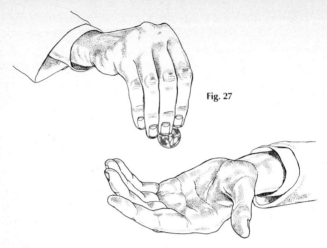

Fig. 27

your right fingers and catch it in the left (Fig. 27). With practice the move will be completely deceptive. The misdirection and cover afforded by the left hand is sufficient to hide it. It is essential that there is no perceptible movement of the right hand – merely a slight relaxation of pressure on the coin by your thumb and forefinger.

Having transferred the coin by this method, carry on rubbing the back of your hand as though the coin were still there. Then slowly raise your right hand to show that the coin has vanished and open your left hand to reveal the coin, which must have penetrated your hand.

The Flight of the Coins

This extremely clever effect was one of Nelson Downs' favourites. Several coins disappear from the left hand and fall into a tumbler one at a time in full view. One gets the impression that the more difficult a trick was to perform, the more he liked it. It probably meant that he had the trick to himself. In addition to a very advanced form of the palm proper, you will need the back palm and also Nelson Downs' own 'Click Pass', which goes like this.

You show several coins in your right hand (Fig. 28) and appear to tip them into your left hand, where apparently they land with a loud click. What actually happens is that as you turn your right hand over to ditch the coins into the waiting palm, you quickly fold the third and fourth fingers into your palm and the coins fall on these with a click (Fig. 29). Then, closing your left hand as though it has received the coins, you move it away, casually drop your right hand, and press the coins into the palm proper. This is not an easy sleight but it is well worth all the practice you will have to put into it.

Back to the trick. In addition to the ability to perform the sleight, you will need a fake – two coins pivotted together – and also a glass tumbler.

You borrow some coins. Nelson Downs managed ten, but I suggest that you restrict your ambition to five, at least to start with. While these are being found, back palm the

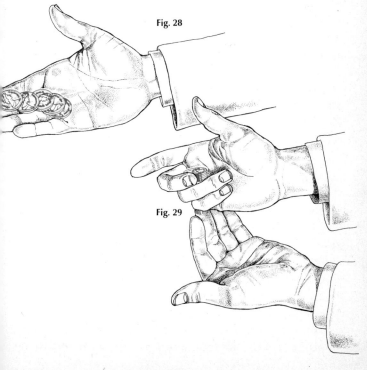

Fig. 28

Fig. 29

Fig. 30 rear view

faked coins in your left hand. Take the borrowed coins into your right hand, showing your left hand to be empty.

As you bring your left hand to your right in order to arrange the coins in readiness for the 'Click Pass', bring the faked coins into your palm as in the usual back and front palm. Now apparently tip the borrowed coins into your left hand but retain them in the right by means of the 'Click Pass'. Close your left hand, as though containing the five coins, and hold it at arm's length. Pick up the tumbler with your right hand as shown in Figure 30. By slightly relaxing the muscles of the palm of the right hand, you can release the coins one at a time so that they fall into the glass. You will need plenty of practice and delicacy of manipulation to ensure that the coins drop singly.

When three coins have fallen into the tumbler, you pretend to hear someone suggest that your left hand is empty. You assure them that the coins do indeed leave your left hand one at a time, and to prove it you show that two coins remain in your left hand. To do this, of course, you separate the pivotted coins. Now let the last two coins fall into the glass and, quickly back palming the faked coins, show your left hand empty.

The Miser's Dream

This is the classic coin routine that can incorporate all the sleights you have learned. The magician appears to produce hundreds of coins from the air to the delight of the audience. Some performers use a top hat; others a borrowed trilby. Some put a saucer inside the hat so that the coins can be heard more clearly; others use champagne buckets that have been specially 'faked' to conceal 'loads' of coins. My own preference is for a large, ordinary tin can. You will also need from twenty to forty coins. About half of these are tied into a pile with fine thread. The remainder are tied into one or two piles and placed in pockets as desired.

Secure the first pile in your left hand and pick up the tin or hat in your right. Show that it is empty. Pass the receptacle to your left hand, holding it with your fingers, covering the coins, on the inside and your thumb on the outside. If using a hat, pick up a saucer and place it inside. Slightly squeeze the coins in your left hand so that the thread breaks and the coins are ready to be released, one at a time.

Reach out with your right hand and appear to grab a coin from the air. Make a throwing movement towards the hat, and at the same time release a coin from your left hand. The sound of the coin falling into the tin, or the saucer, completes the illusion of a coin being produced. Take the coin out and show it. Then apparently throw it back again, actually palming it and releasing another coin from your left hand.

Now, unknown to the audience, you have a coin palmed in your right hand. You appear to see another coin in the air, reach out, and catch it. Show it clearly and once more appear to throw it into the tin. Continue in this way until all the coins have been dropped from the left hand.

The manner of catching and throwing the coins should be varied as much as possible. You could appear to throw some coins through the base of the tin; some could be thrown into the air and caught as they fall, the sound coming of course from coins dropped from your left hand.

One very effective idea is to pretend to put a coin in your mouth, actually palming it of course, and appear to blow it into the tin.

When you have, say, twenty coins in the tin, dip your right hand in, take out a handful, and pour them back again. Do this several times as you walk amongst the audience. Finally pour a handful back, but retain seven or eight, which can be produced from behind a spectator's lapel. Pretend to throw these into the tin but actually strike the edge sharply with your wrist so that the contents jump and make a loud clatter. Properly timed, this is a perfect illusion. You can now produce the coins, which have been retained in your right hand, from a hat or anywhere else that takes your fancy.

By introducing the other bundles of coins during the routine, you will end up with the number supposed to have been caught. These can finally be tipped into a glass receptacle, bringing the effect to a very satisfactory and somewhat noisy climax.

Coin Magic with Special Apparatus

More progress has been made in the production of trick coins and special apparatus for coin magic than for any other branch of the art. Described here are many of the more standard pieces of apparatus. To keep abreast of all the latest developments, one should obtain the catalogues published by magic-dealers. We begin, however, with three tricks requiring apparatus that you can easily make yourself.

A trick matchbox
A large coin is placed in a matchbox, which is then closed. When the box is reopened, the coin is found to have disappeared. The performer shows empty hands and proceeds to tear the box to shreds, thus proving beyond all doubt that the coin is no longer there.

To perform this trick you will need a specially faked matchbox. Make it by carefully cutting the bottom from the drawer of a matchbox. This will later help to form a double bottom to an ordinary, complete matchbox.

At the start of the trick the extra bottom, or flap, is held between the outer cover and the drawer, which is pushed out slightly. When you open the box to receive the coin, you must prevent the flap from dropping by holding it with your thumb (Fig. 31). Borrow a coin and have it placed in the matchbox. Close the box, whereupon the flap falls and covers the coin. You may now shake the box up and down to prove that the coin really is inside.

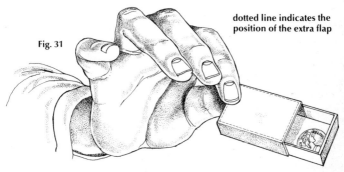

Fig. 31

dotted line indicates the position of the extra flap

After a mystic wave of your hand, or the utterance of a magic word, you again shake the box: silence – the coin has gone! But this time you are shaking the box from side to side to side, not up and down as before, and simultaneously applying pressure from the sides. The coin will not rattle as it has not sufficient room to move in a lateral direction. The audience assumes that the coin has left the box.

When you remove the drawer and show it empty, the spectators are absolutely convinced the coin is no longer there. The flap covering the coin is a perfect match for the real bottom of the matchbox and your hands are demonstrably empty. You now carelessly throw the outer cover to a member of the audience for examination and proceed to demolish the drawer, beginning with the sides.

As you do this, allow the coin to slide out onto one hand

and either finger palm it or, better still, press it into the palm proper. While it remains hidden, you complete the destruction of the matchbox by tearing it into little pieces. You can bring the trick to a satisfactory climax by reproducing the coin from some totally unexpected place.

A trick pillbox

You can also vanish a coin using a cardboard pillbox. These are easily obtainable in various sizes from a chemist or drug store. First decide what coin you are going to use because the size of the pillbox depends upon this. The diameter of the inside of the box must be such that, when the coin is placed inside, it will exactly cover the bottom. Line the box with a brightly coloured paper and cover one side of the coin with matching paper.

To perform, you first pass the empty box out for examination. Secretly take the prepared coin from a convenient pocket, borrow a coin, and switch it for your faked one by means of the 'De Manche Change'. Show the prepared coin to the audience, with of course the covered side towards yourself. Drop it into the box papered-side uppermost. As in the last trick, shake the box up and down to rattle the coin and prove that it is indeed in there. To make it disappear, after a few mystic passes, simply shake the box from side to side, putting on a little pressure with your fingers, and the coin will be silent.

The audience will assume that the box is empty and this is confirmed when you allow spectators to look inside – the coin cannot be seen. Close the box once more, and, after more mystic passes, open it up and turn the coin out on your palm. The box can be examined again and, having made the switch for the original coin, this may be passed back to its owner.

The Coin Cone

A coin is borrowed and marked. A glass tumbler is also shown and placed mouth downwards on a table. Next a paper cover with a hole right through it is shown and placed over the tumbler. The performer now drops the borrowed coin into the cover so that it lands with a clink upon the upturned glass. After a few mystical waves, the cover is lifted from the glass to show that the coin has gone from the base and can now be seen resting on the table under the glass. Picking up the coin, the performer then makes it vanish, only to reproduce it from a nest of boxes, an orange, or some other hiding place.

The secret lies in the special construction of the paper or cardboard cone. This must be large enough to fit over the glass and have a partition glued into it near the top. The partition has a small hole cut in it and is fixed at such a height as to rest on the bottom of the inverted glass when the cone is placed over it (Fig. 32). You will also need the glass tumbler, of course, and a duplicate coin.

Give the glass out for examination while you borrow a coin. Have the coin marked. Next show the paper cone and explain that it is hollow all the way through. To prove this point you should pass a wand or pencil through it: an easy matter because the partition has a hole in it.

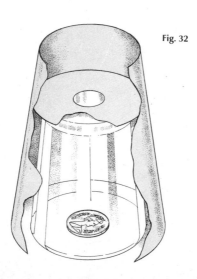

Fig. 32

Place the inverted glass on the table and cover it with the cone. As you do this, however, you introduce the duplicate coin under the glass. This may sound difficult but is quite simple in practice. The action can be performed with one or both hands while the audience is misdirected to the borrowed coin.

Drop the borrowed coin into the top of the cone, where it lands, unbeknown to your audience, on the partition. When the cover is lifted, the coin comes with it, and the duplicate is shown on the table. You now proceed to tear up the cover, secretly obtaining and palming the marked coin as you do so. Then you simply change the marked coin for the duplicate and pass it out for examination. Alternatively you could make the duplicate coin disappear and cause it to 'reappear' in some piece of apparatus, this latter one being the original marked coin that you had palmed in the course of the trick and loaded at a convenient moment.

The Shell Coin

One of the most versatile trick coins is known as a 'shell coin'. This is a coin that has been hollowed out, leaving only a thin shell of metal which fits over another coin. To casual inspection it will pass as an ordinary single coin, but, by slipping the solid coin out of the shell, it becomes to all appearances two coins (Fig. 33). Dozens of tricks can be performed with a shell coin, such as, for instance, the following, which is called 'The Escaping Coin'.

shell   Fig. 33

solid

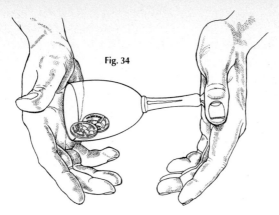

Fig. 34

duplicate coin palmed in this hand

A wine glass and two coins are shown. The coins are placed into the glass, one at a time. The performer then puts the right hand over the mouth of the glass, the left on the bottom, and asks the audience if it is possible for one of the coins to escape without the hand moving from the mouth of the glass. Once the audience is agreed that it would be impossible, the performer gives the glass a slight shake and one of the coins disappears and finds its way through the foot of the glass into the left hand.

In beginning the trick, you place the two 'coins' within the horizontal glass, resting them on the side with the shell coin slightly overlapping the solid one. In your left hand you have palmed an ordinary duplicate coin. This is covered and kept securely against the foot of the glass when you hold it as shown in Figure 34.

When you want the coin to vanish, all you do is give the glass a slight shake and at the same time bring it to a vertical position. This will cause the shell to slip over the solid so that they appear to be a single coin. You now raise the glass and show the palmed coin, which has apparently passed clean through the bottom. Coins and glass may be passed out for inspection, providing you palm off the shell before handing out the faked coin.

The Stack of Coins

This extremely clever gimmick can be purchased from most magic-dealers. It consists of five coins riveted together near one edge. The centres of the lower four coins are drilled away but the topmost coin is left intact (Fig. 35). Because only one pin is used to rivet them together, it acts as a pivot and the coins may be casually spread to show that they are quite 'normal'. Stacked, they appear to be simply a pile of coins. When the stack of coins was originally placed on the market, it came complete with a brass cap with which to cover the coins. The modern version does away with the cap as it looks too gimmicky. Many routines can be devised using this apparatus. Here is one.

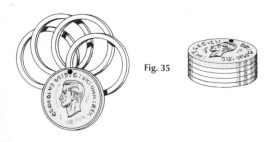

Fig. 35

Five coins are borrowed from members of the audience. The performer makes a little tube by rolling up a piece of paper and then blocks one end by twisting the paper together. A small die is placed upon the table and covered with the paper tube. Then the performer picks up the coins one at a time and passes them magically under the cover. This is now lifted to reveal the coins, the die having disappeared. The cover is replaced over the coins and they are apparently caused to pass right through the table into the performer's hand because, when the cover is lifted again, the coins have indeed departed and the die has returned in their place.

Before the routine begins, the paper tube must be prepared by rolling it round the stack of coins and marking it with a pencil to indicate how far it must go to make a tube which will just fit easily – neither too loosely or too tightly – over the coins. Place the stack in your right-hand coat or trouser pocket where you can easily secure it unseen by the audience.

First borrow the five coins from members of your audience and place them upon the table in a heap, trying to match the top coin as closely as possible to the top coin of your stack. Now take out the die and place it down by the coins. Show the piece of paper and roll it into a tube, taking care to roll it exactly to the mark you have already drawn so that it will just fit over the coins. Twist the paper to close it at one end and show it to the spectators to prove it is quite free of deception. On returning to the table, finger palm the stack from your pocket and slip it into the tube. This is the work of a moment and, with practice, you will find you can do it quite unseen by the audience.

You now place the paper tube, with the stack hidden inside it, over the die. Pick up one of the coins and make it disappear by means of the 'French Drop'. Make a pass over the paper cover. Repeat this operation with each of the coins until all five are palmed in your hand. Great care must be taken not to allow the coins to clink against each other as each new coin is pressed above the others into your palm.

Raise the paper cover and reveal the stack. If the die is small, the coins may be spread very slightly as you count them to emphasize that all five coins have arrived. Replace the paper cover over the stack. Saying that you will now pass the coins through the table, you take the hand containing the palmed coins beneath the table and knock sharply, allowing the coins to clink as loudly as possible. Bringing the hand instantly into view again, you throw the five coins onto the table. Now raise the paper cover, holding it near the bottom and pinching it sufficiently to carry the stack away with it, thus revealing the die once more. As you carelessly toss the paper cover into the audience, allow the weight of the stack to make it fall straight into the finger palm. The stack can be ditched later at an opportune moment.

This is one of my favourite tricks. When available, I often use the drawer taken from a box of matches in preference to the paper tube. This is just as obviously unprepared and makes for neater handling.

The See-Through Coin Cap

Let me now introduce you to a beautiful piece of apparatus that you can obtain from a good magic-dealer.

It consists of a small brass cap of sufficient diameter exactly to cover the coin to be used and of sufficient depth to take three coins. One of the coins, however, is very special. It has been filed down to half its thickness and has a brass disc, exactly resembling the inside of the cap, soldered to it; also a hole has been drilled right through the centre of the special coin exactly coinciding with one in the cap (Fig. 36). When the special coin is placed in the cap with the brass side outwards, it is impossible to detect its presence and one can still see through the cap. So neatly does the faked coin fit the cap that the apparatus can be handed out for examination with no fear of discovery. To remove the coin, it is necessary to dislodge it by banging the cap smartly down upon a table.

Fig. 36

brass disc

coin

You first hand out the cap alone for examination, drawing attention to the fact that the spectators can see right through it. Next you take three coins from your pocket, one of which is the faked one. Show the coins quite freely but make sure the underside of the faked coin is kept out of sight. Place the three coins on the extended fingers of your left hand, the faked coin on top, brass side down of course.

Cover the three coins with the cap, using sufficient pressure to force the faked coin well home. All you have to do is raise the cap and one of the coins has vanished completely. To prove the point beyond all doubt, your audience can see clear through the cap: a superb piece of apparatus, I think you will agree.

The Coin Wand

You may have some difficulty in obtaining a coin wand as it has become something of a collector's item. Nevertheless, it is an interesting piece of apparatus that you should know about.

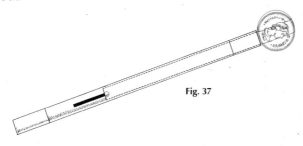

Fig. 37

To all intents and purposes the wand is just the usual magician's emblem. It has, however, the additional ability to produce a coin instantly at the end of it. The wand is in fact a hollow metal tube with a coin inside it. The coin has been cut into three sections across its face and reunited with a spring. Divided in this way, the coin fits snugly inside the wand. It folds up as it is drawn into the wand and rapidly expands when forced out. These movements are controlled by a sliding stud that protrudes from a slot in the side of the wand and is worked by the performer's thumb (Fig. 37). The coin wand provides a nice diversion in routines like the classic 'Miser's Dream'.

The Penetrating Coin

The performer borrows a coin and a hat, saying that he or she will pass the coin right through the crown of the hat. Proceeding to do this, the performer stops halfway, showing the coin half inside and half outside, and then draws the coin right through the hat. Next a teacup is shown, the hat is put on it crown downwards, and three coins are borrowed. The performer then throws the coins into the hat and one of them passes right through the crown and is heard to fall into the teacup below.

For this one you need a special trick coin. It is grooved all around the edge to take a small rubber band and divided horizontally into two equal portions, the point of a fine

Fig. 38

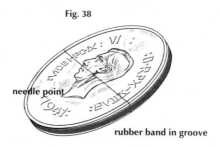

needle point

rubber band in groove

needle being fixed to the top half (Fig. 38). The rubber band holds the two halves together when open or folded.

Palm the trick coin in your left hand and borrow a hat, which you also hold in your left hand. Next borrow a coin. Take it in your right hand and place it inside the hat. Pretend to push the coin through the hat from the inside, pressing the top of the hat against your left hand. Under cover of this hand, bend the trick coin in half and push the needle point down into the hat so that the coin appears to protrude halfway through (Fig. 39). Pull it clear, whereupon it will immediately spring flat to become a 'whole' coin again.

All you have to do now is switch it for the borrowed coin and return it to the owner. The trick coin can be disposed

Fig. 39

of at your convenience but at the same time take the opportunity to steal an ordinary coin. This you will need for the second effect.

You borrow back the hat and, in placing it crown downwards on top of the cup, you secretly introduce the coin between the crown of the hat and the edge of the teacup (Fig. 40). This will need practice but is not too difficult to accomplish. Borrow three more coins, and, taking them in your right hand, position one of them in the palm proper. Appear to throw all three coins forcibly into the hat, actually retaining the one in the palm proper. The impact

dotted line indicates the position of the palmed coin

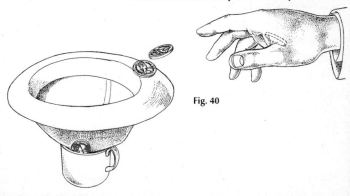

Fig. 40

of the coins hitting the inside of the hat causes it to move slightly, which dislodges the hidden coin and allows it to fall audibly into the cup.

The Drilled Coin

The magician borrows a coin and appears to drill a hole right through its centre with a forefinger.

You will need a coin which has had a hole large enough to take your forefinger drilled clean through it. Finger palm this in your left hand as you borrow a coin. Place the borrowed coin in your left-hand fingers, secretly bringing the fake coin in front of it. As far as the audience is concerned, you are only holding the borrowed coin.

Push your right forefinger through the hole in the special coin with a twisting movement as though drilling. As you 'penetrate' the coin, your forefinger pushes the borrowed coin into the left finger-palm position. Show the coin on your finger. By reversing the above moves, you extract your forefinger and bring the borrowed coin up against the fake coin once more. As you go to return the ordinary coin, slide off the fake coin, and palm it until it can be ditched.

Some magic-dealers sell the fake coin used for this trick with an extra shell coin to cover it. This is, of course, similar to the shell coin already described on page 106. The moves are much the same as above but this coin has the advantage of being only single-coin thickness and is therefore more deceptive.

Yet another trick coin for this effect has the centre cut out but the resultant hole is filled by a disc of exactly the right size cut from another coin. This disc is spring hinged so that the finger, or a pencil, can be pushed through but on removal it closes instantly.

The Coin Cylinder

When 'The Yellow Perils' were written, the coin cylinder was made of brass. Nowadays a perfectly acceptable and

Fig. 41

recess to hold one coin

efficient one can be obtained in plastic. The secret lies in the fact that on the underside of the cylinder is a recess that is just deep enough to hold one coin (Fig. 41). When turned bottom upwards with a coin in position, the cylinder appears to be filled with coins, and on this fact depends the effect of another coin vanish.

You give the cylinder out for examination and request the loan of six coins. While this is going on, you calmly slip your hand into a pocket and bring out an extra coin, hidden in the palm proper. You collect up the borrowed coins in your left hand and transfer them to the right hand, thereby adding them to the palmed coin. You now have seven coins in your hand instead of six, but this will not be noticed.

Pick up the cylinder in your left hand and put it down carelessly upon the heap of coins in your right hand; in so doing, cover one of the coins and slip it into the recess. Next pile the coins into the cylinder one at a time, counting them aloud. With one finger underneath the cylinder holding the concealed coin in place, transfer it to your left hand, ostensibly to show your right hand empty. As you do this, however, you secretly turn the cylinder over, bringing the recessed side and the hidden coin uppermost. You again take the cylinder in your right hand, leaving the pile of coins in the left, firmly held between the second and third joints of the fingers.

The cylinder still appears to be holding six coins. A spectator is asked to cover the cylinder for a moment with a handkerchief. Under cover of this, you quickly reverse the cylinder and, when the handkerchief is withdrawn, it is seen to be 'empty'. You now pass your left hand up behind your right elbow and, seizing the cloth at the sleeve, give it a slight shake and allow the six palmed coins to fall upon the table. It appears that they have been miraculously extracted from your elbow. You can now hand out the cylinder for examination, the extra coin being retained in the finger palm and dropped into a convenient pocket while your audience is misdirected to the apparatus.

The Rattle Box

A standard piece of apparatus for vanishing a coin is the 'rattle box'. This is a small, oblong wooden box with a sliding lid and a false bottom. From the outside it appears twice as deep as the inside actually is, and the end of the lid is made to fit flush with the false bottom of the box. With the lid not quite closed, if a coin is placed in the box and the box held in a slanting position, the coin will slide out into your hand (Fig. 42). To provide the necessary misdirection, a small piece of metal is inserted in the false base. This is held by a spring which can be released by pressure on the bottom of the box at the rear.

Fig. 42

In performance you place a coin, which may be borrowed, into the box. As you close the box, you tip it slightly and allow the coin to slide out at the back into your hand, where it is palmed. To 'prove' that the coin is still in the box, you give it a shake. By applying pressure on the bottom, the piece of metal is released and rattles away merrily, completely misleading your audience. In due course, releasing pressure on the box will stop the rattling and the box can be shown empty – the coin has disappeared. In the meantime, of course, you will have placed the coin ready for the denouement.

The Multiplying Coin Tray

This is a standard piece of apparatus obtainable from most magic-dealers and even appears in cabinets of simple conjuring tricks.

Back in the days of 'The Yellow Perils', these trays were made in japanned tin; these days they are produced in plastic. The tray or plate has a slot hidden in its base which can take three or four coins (Fig. 43). If a few coins are counted onto the tray and then tipped into the hands of a member of the audience, or directly into an empty pocket, you can secretly add the hidden coins.

Fig. 43

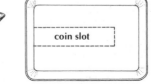

coin slot

This can be made into a complete trick very simply. Hide three coins in the slot. Borrow seven coins and have them counted onto the tray. Tip the coins directly into someone's pocket. Now show three more coins. Take these one at a time and by means of the 'French Drop' make them disappear. When the coins are removed from the pocket and counted, it will be found that the three coins have joined the original seven by magic.

The Coin Tumbler

A useful piece of apparatus in coin magic is a tumbler which has a slot cut in its side near the bottom. Coins dropped inside make their escape through the slot. Here is a trick using such a tumbler.

The magician borrows a coin and has it marked for later identification. He or she drops the coin in a glass tumbler, which is then covered with a handkerchief and placed upon a china plate. Next another tumbler is picked up and shown to be empty. The plate and its burden are then placed upon the second tumbler (Fig. 44). The magician takes a corner of the handkerchief and pulls it suddenly away. At this moment the coin is seen and heard to drop into the lower tumbler. The coin is tipped out of the tumbler and returned to its owner.

Apart from the coin tumbler, you need a duplicate coin attached by means of a blob of wax to the centre of the

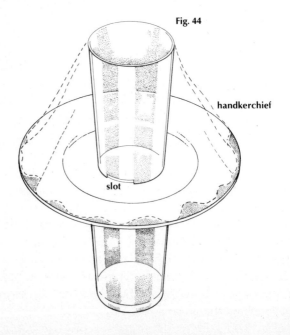

Fig. 44

handkerchief

slot

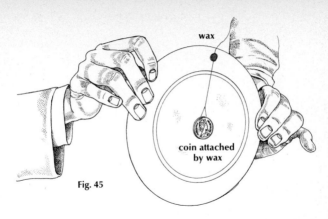

wax

coin attached
by wax

Fig. 45

bottom of the plate (Fig. 45). To do this, you must press a small wafer of wax to the bottom of the plate, lay a loop of thread over it, and then press the coin on top. When the thread is pulled, the loop will cut through the wax and release the coin. This is a useful dodge that you may well find helpful in other effects. The thread runs to the edge of the plate, where you should make a big knot and fix it with a spot of wax.

Drop the borrowed coin into the faked tumbler and cover it with a handkerchief. Shake the tumbler to let the audience hear that the coin is indeed within. Then let it slide through the slot into your hand. Next put the covered tumbler on the prepared plate and in turn pick this up and place it on top of the other tumbler. The coin is finger palmed in your right hand.

Hold the edge of the plate firmly in your left hand to steady it and take hold of the handkerchief by one corner, together with the knot on the thread. The plate should have been positioned so that the knot is nearest to you. A firm, steady pull will release the coin and carry the handkerchief clear of the upper tumbler. The coin drops with a clink into the lower tumbler and the trick is almost complete. Pick up the tumbler in your left hand and tip the coin into your right palm, where it stays. Push the finger-palmed, marked coin up to your fingertips and return it for identification.

HANDKERCHIEF MAGIC

The production of brightly coloured silk handkerchiefs is a very popular effect and, with the addition of two or three other handkerchief tricks, can easily become the basis of a complete act. Back in the early 1900s George Stillwell performed a very elaborate and successful silk act. I can think of no better way to start this chapter on handkerchief magic than to describe his opening sleight.

Production of Silks

The magician shows both hands unmistakably empty, back and front. Then, with the left hand, one silk after another is produced from the tips of the fingers of the right hand.

In addition to learning the sleight, you will need a small rubber or plastic ball, hollow with a hole in the side. You push three silk handkerchiefs into this fake, hooking the end of each silk to the next to facilitate their subsequent removal. To perform the sleight, you will first need to learn to retain the ball in the palm proper as already described on page 74. Secondly, you must be able to pass the ball secretly from the palm of one hand to that of the other.

The move is as follows. Facing half left, with the loaded ball palmed in your right hand, bring it up to your obviously empty left hand and, as your palms cross, press the ball into your left hand in the palm-proper position and retain it there. Now turn to face half right, bringing the back of your left hand, containing the palmed ball, and the empty palm of your right hand towards the audience. Reverse these movements and the ball is again hidden in your right-hand palm-proper position.

To continue the action, quickly bring your right hand up to your left (Fig. 1), catch hold of the corner of the first handkerchief between your left thumb and forefinger, and pull your right hand sharply downwards so that the silk suddenly appears as though plucked from your right-hand fingertips (Fig. 2). Place this first silk between your left first and second fingers (Fig. 3).

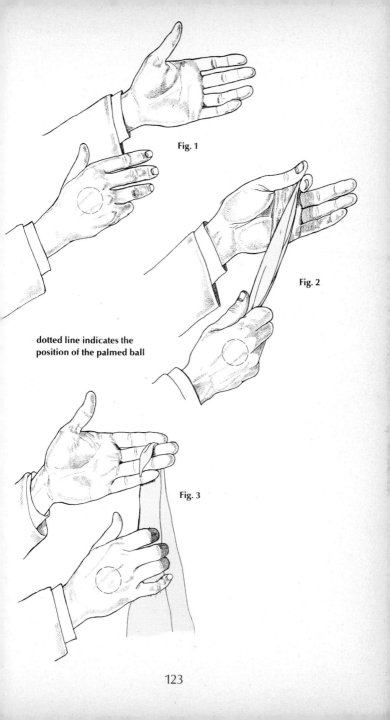

Fig. 1

Fig. 2

dotted line indicates the
position of the palmed ball

Fig. 3

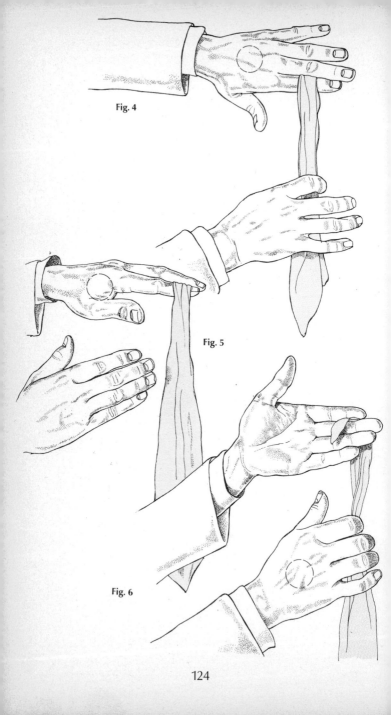

Fig. 4

Fig. 5

Fig. 6

124

In order to show both hands empty, there follows a variation on the change-over palm sleight already described. Bring your right hand up to your left and transfer the ball from palm to palm. Immediately turn the back of your left hand to the audience, and, flipping the handkerchief over the back of your fingers, stroke it down with your right hand (Fig. 4). This hand can now be shown empty. Bring your right hand up to the left, which is immediately turned (Fig. 5), and palm the ball into your right hand once more. Stroke the silk, again with your right hand, but this time it conceals the ball (Fig. 6).

To produce the second handkerchief, you go back to the beginning of the action, and so on for the third. If you sew a tiny bead in one corner of each silk handkerchief, you will find it much easier to locate the ends and pull them singly from the ball.

Producing Eggs from a Handkerchief

This is a good old favourite which you will enjoy doing. The magician borrows a hat and places it down on a chair or table. Next he or she takes a large handkerchief from a pocket and displays it by holding it up by two of its corners. It is folded once, and when given a shake out tumbles a real egg into the hat. The process is repeated again and again and the trick is brought to a close by distributing the eggs to members of the audience and allowing the hat and handkerchief to be examined.

You will need half a dozen or so eggs and two large handkerchiefs. Blow one of the eggs and make a small hole at one end and a larger hole at the other. Thread a large darning needle with thin black cotton and tie a very large knot at the end of the thread. Pass the needle through the larger of the two holes, drawing the thread through the egg until the large knot reaches the smaller hole. Fix the free end of the thread to the centre of the hem at the edge of one of the handkerchiefs. (Let's call that edge AB.) The length of the thread must be such that it allows the egg to dangle just a little below the centre of the handkerchief (Fig. 7).

Carefully fold this handkerchief, with the egg inside, and put it in a convenient place. Put the unprepared handkerchief, rolled up small and held by an elastic band, in the bottom of your right-hand coat pocket. Now divide up the eggs you are going to produce, putting some in your left pocket and some in your right pocket, on top of the duplicate handkerchief.

Borrow a hat and, as you return to your table, load it with an egg. Place the hat crown downwards on the table. Carefully pull out the prepared handkerchief, making sure that the blown egg hangs down on the side away from the audience. Bring Corners A and B together in your left hand (Fig. 8) and, passing your right hand down the edges of the handkerchief, take hold of Corners C and D (Fig. 9). The egg now lies between the two halves of the doubled-up handkerchief. Drop Corners A and B, take Corner C in your right hand, drawing this away from Corner D, which is still held in your left hand, and the egg will fall out into the hat.

Make sure the audience have a good view of the falling egg, and hold the handkerchief sufficiently high for the egg not actually to hit the bottom of the inside of the hat or it may break (Fig. 10). Immediately drape the handkerchief over the hat, with Corners C and D resting on the table at

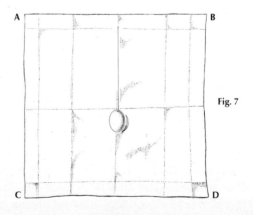

Fig. 7

Fig. 8

Fig. 9

Fig. 10

the front and Corners A and B resting on the brim at either side.

Remove the real egg from the hat, take it into the audience, and hand it to one of the spectators. On returning to your table, load another egg into the hat as you pick up the handkerchief again by Corners A and B. This brings you back to the starting position, and you can continue to produce eggs in this way until all the stock is used up.

On producing the last egg, let the faked handkerchief fall into the hat. Take this last egg into the audience, and on your return secure the duplicate handkerchief from your right pocket and drop it into the hat as you 'feel for other eggs'. During this action, crumple up the faked handkerchief and blown egg into your left hand. Next take the hat and duplicate handkerchief into the audience for examination, casually place your left hand in a pocket, and ditch the faked handkerchief.

Although no difficult sleight of hand is called for in this trick, a measure of neat handling is necessary which will only come from much practice.

Silks and Soup Plates

This is another classical effect much beloved by magicians throughout the ages.

The magician lays a newspaper on the seat of a chair and places a soup plate upon it. Two brightly coloured silk handkerchiefs are shown and rolled into the hand, one at a time. Each time the hand is passed over the plate and each time the handkerchief disappears. When both have vanished, the soup plate is raised and they are discovered beneath it.

You will need two red silk handkerchiefs and two green ones, a newspaper, a soup plate, a small 'servante' fixed behind a chair, and a standard 'silk vanisher'. A servante is a small shelf which can be hooked behind a table or chair to enable the magician to secure or ditch an object secretly as required. The silk vanisher consists of a small receptacle made of metal or plastic, joined to which is a length of black elastic. The free end of the elastic is attached by means of a safety pin to the inside back of the coat. So that it may be easily secured, the receptacle is lodged in a right-hand coat pocket or wedged in the trouser band on that side.

The newspaper is fitted with a pocket, made by gluing a square of newspaper near the edge of one side and leaving one end open. Into this pocket go one red and one green handkerchief. The paper is folded in half with the pocket in between. The remaining handkerchiefs are on view on the table.

Open the paper and show it to the audience with the pocket side away from them. Refold the paper and hold it in your left hand with the pocket still on the side away from the audience. Now pick up the soup plate in your right hand and show it. Place the soup plate, back outwards, in your left hand, grasping it with your thumb against the newspaper and your fingers beneath it. Now take the newspaper in your right hand at the bottom edge, draw it away, and lay it down upon the seat of the chair. As you do this, slip the handkerchiefs out of the pocket in the paper so that they are now concealed behind the plate. Lay the plate upon the newspaper on the chair with the handkerchiefs secretly hidden beneath it.

Take one of the handkerchiefs from the table by its centre and hang it over the open palm of your left hand. Using your flat, open right hand, rub the silk between the palms of your hands in a circular motion, the hands going in opposite directions. This will cause the silk to roll up into a ball. Pretend to place this in your right hand but in reality leave it in the left, immediately picking up a wand in this hand so helping to conceal the palmed handkerchief.

Hold your closed right hand over the plate and touch the hand with the wand. Open the hand and show that the silk has disappeared. As you turn to pick up the second silk, ditch the palmed handkerchief into a pocket. Transfer the second silk to your left hand and turn your body half right to show it to the audience on that side. Under cover of this move, secure the vanisher in your right hand.

Turn to the left again and bring your right hand, closed into a fist, in front of you and cover it with the handkerchief. This time as you rub your hands together you work the silk into the vanisher. Draw attention to the end of the silk just before it is completely pushed inside, and then give it a final push and, under cover of your hands, part your wrists and release the vanisher. It will fly instantly out of sight under your coat and come to rest near the small of your back. Continue the rubbing movement for a second or two. Then open your hands to show that the silk has completely disappeared.

Raise the plate and reveal that the handkerchiefs have been magically transported beneath it.

The Vanishing Knots

The magician holds a silk handkerchief at its centre with both hands and requests a member of the audience to tie a knot. Saying that it is not tight enough, the performer gives the ends a tug. Then another spectator, and another, are asked to tie knots. Eventually half a dozen knots have been tied and each one tightened by the magician. The knots are covered with a loose end of the handkerchief and it is handed to someone to hold. However, as soon as it reaches the spectator's hands, the magician asks that it be shaken out: the knots have all disappeared.

This is a very effective little trick and makes a nice prelude to something more ambitious using the same handkerchief. Instead of tightening the knot in each case, all you have to do is pull on one end only, straightening it from its twisted position, so that it becomes a slip knot. With all the knots treated in this way, it is a simple matter, under cover of the loose end, to draw the straightened part right out of the slip knots so that the handkerchief can be shaken and shown to be knotless.

The All-Change Silk

Many magicians have performed this trick over the years, most notably David Devant. All had their own versions and the one that follows is a good example.

The magician asks for a handkerchief and, while one is being found, produces a lemon from someone's coat. The borrowed handkerchief is then rolled into a small ball which is given to someone to hold with the promise that it will disappear. But, when after a few moments it is still seen to be there, the magician asks that it be unfolded and returned to its owner. However, on being undone, the handkerchief is found to be in pieces.

The magician is aghast, blames the spectator for squeezing the handkerchief too hard, but says that it will be returned to its original condition by magic. The pieces are taken and rubbed between the hands; then they are passed to a helper with the request that he or she continue to rub the pieces together. After a moment or two the performer again takes the bundle and, on unrolling it, finds that it has now been converted into one long strip.

The magician apologizes for the mistake, rolls the strip into a ball, and pushes it into a loaded pistol. The pistol is fired in the direction of the lemon, which is then picked up and cut open to reveal the handkerchief in one piece again. Saying that it smells of lemon, the magician places it upon a plate and sprinkles it with perfume from a bottle. But as the bottle is put away, a mischievious assistant, who is standing behind holding a lighted candle, leans forward and sets the handkerchief on fire.

The magician scolds the assistant and, blowing out the flame, goes off-stage for a moment, returning with a sheet of paper in which the burnt remains are wrapped. The parcel is then offered to the owner of the handkerchief, who naturally enough refuses to accept it and demands recompense for the loss. However, all is well as the magician rips open the parcel and brings forth the spectator's handkerchief in perfect condition.

In addition to the borrowed handkerchief, you will need a few pieces of cambric, a long strip of cambric, a candle, a bottle of perfume, and a plate. You will also need to paste two squares of paper together around three sides so as to form a bag. Finally you must have a lemon, from which you cut a circular plug and remove the pulp. Into this hollow lemon you place an ordinary cambric handkerchief and replace the plug. You will have to fasten this with a piece of wire. Position the bundle of pieces, the long strip, and the lemon in easily accessible places, e.g. in pockets, in your waistband, or behind a piece of apparatus on your table.

First ask for the loan of a handkerchief and at the same time palm the lemon. Produce the lemon from someone's person. Secure the bundle of pieces and, on rolling the borrowed handkerchief into a ball, make a switch, handing the bundle of pieces to a spectator to hold. On returning to your table, ditch the borrowed handkerchief into a pocket and palm out the long strip.

In accordance with the routine already described, roll the bundle of pieces in your hands and take the opportunity to switch it for the long strip. This is pushed into the barrel of the pistol and left there. The handkerchief removed from the lemon is really burnt. When you run off-stage to get the square of paper, you quickly slip the borrowed handkerchief into the secret pocket in it. Then, having wrapped the burnt pieces in the paper, all you have to do to remove the handkerchief is break open one layer of the paper and draw it out.

The Twentieth-Century Silks

There is a classic handkerchief trick said to have been invented and first performed by David Devant at the Egyptian Hall in London.

A blue and a yellow silk handkerchief are tied together, rolled into a ball, and placed in a glass tumbler. The magician then puts a red silk handkerchief into a glass tube,

where it remains in full view of the audience. Suddenly the red handkerchief disappears and is found tied between the blue and yellow handkerchiefs in the glass.

For this great effect you will need a glass tumbler, a cylindrical glass or perspex tube approximately 8 inches (20.32 cm) long and about 2 inches (5.08 cm) in diameter, a diamond-shaped handkerchief with a red centre and a blue border, and three square silk handkerchiefs with contrasting coloured borders. The yellow handkerchief has a blue border, the blue handkerchief has a yellow border, and the third is red with a blue border.

The blue border of the yellow handkerchief is opened about $\frac{1}{2}$ inch (1.27 cm) from one corner. The diamond-shaped handkerchief is tied with a very small knot to the corner near the opening and is pushed inside the border until it is out of sight except for its blue corner. The yellow handkerchief should now appear quite normal because the tiny piece of the blue border of the diamond-shaped red handkerchief which shows is the same colour as the border of the yellow one (Fig. 11).

In addition to all this equipment, you will need a 'pull'. This is an arrangement using a length of nylon string and a small strap which enables the performer to vanish small

Fig. 11   corner of the concealed handkerchief

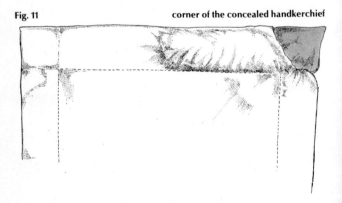

objects. The strap is buckled around your left arm just above the wrist and one end of the string is securely attached to it. The string passes up your sleeve through one ring attached to your coat with a safety pin at the left armpit, through a second ring attached in the same manner at your right armpit, and down to your right cuff, where it ends in a loop which is hooked onto a cuff link or button so as to be readily accessible when required.

To perform, pick up the blue and yellow handkerchiefs and display them. Then appear to tie them together but in reality tie one yellow corner of the blue silk to the small blue corner of the red silk, which lies hidden inside the border of the yellow silk. Show them apparently knotted (Fig. 12). Roll these handkerchiefs up and place them in the glass, which you either put on the table or give to someone to hold.

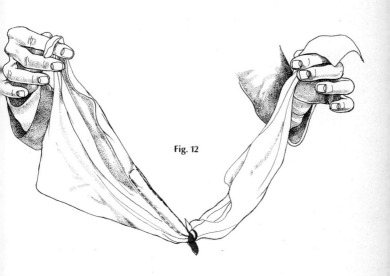

Fig. 12

**handkerchief on the right is knotted
to the corner of the concealed handkerchief**

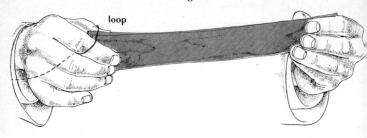

Fig. 13

loop

As you return to your performing position, secretly remove the loop from your cuff link or button and slide it over the thumb and forefinger of your right hand. Pick up the red silk with your left hand at one corner and hold the opposite corner in your right hand. Now fold the hand- kerchief over and over to make a narrow strip and slip the loop just over the end in your right hand (Fig. 13). Then, with your left hand, take this end and pull it through until the loop is in the centre (Fig. 14). Let go of both ends on completion of this movement so that the red handkerchief is now doubled through the loop in your right hand.

Pick up the glass cylinder in your left hand and show it. Next push the red handkerchief into the centre of the cylinder, using your right forefinger (Fig. 15). Now take the cylinder between your hands, the ends resting on your open palms. Ask the audience to watch the silk and, with an upward movement of both elbows, you cause the pull to draw the handkerchief right out of the tube and up your right sleeve (Fig. 16). You will find with practice that the handkerchief goes so quickly that your audience will have no clue as to its whereabouts.

All that is left is to remove the two handkerchiefs from the glass and pull them apart sharply by their extreme corners, whereupon the hidden red silk is pulled out of its hiding place and appears tied between the two handker- chiefs as if by magic.

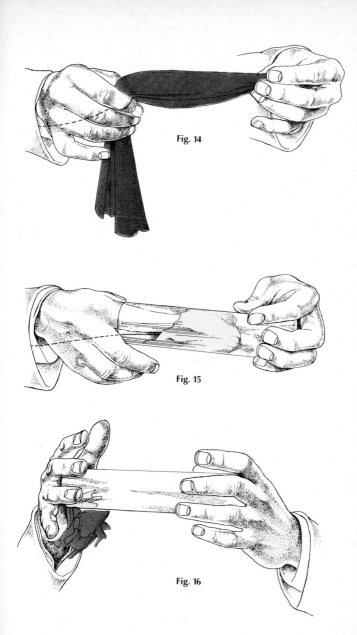

Fig. 14

Fig. 15

Fig. 16

The Colour-Changing Silks

The magician shows a small sheet of white paper, rolls it into a tube, and secures it with an elastic band. Two white silk handkerchiefs are then shown and placed into one end of the paper tube. On being withdrawn from the other end, they are seen to have changed colour: one red, one blue.

You will require a special gimmick in the form of a metal or plastic tube approximately 4 inches (10.16 cm) long and $1\frac{1}{2}$ inches (3.81 cm) in diameter. The tube is fitted with a small cloth bag, which is normally sewn by its mouth into the centre of the tube via holes bored in it. You will also need two white, one blue, and one red silk handkerchief, all of the same size, a sheet of stiff white card approximately 9 inches (22.86 cm) square, and a small elastic band. The red handkerchief is sewn at its centre to the bottom of the cloth bag (Fig. 17).

To prepare, the attached red silk must be pushed into the gimmick, followed by the blue one, so that they are completely hidden and prevented from emerging from the other end by means of the cloth bag. Lay one of the white handkerchiefs bunched up upon the table and on it the gimmick. The end into which the handkerchiefs were pushed should be towards the back of the table. Throw the second white handkerchief over the front end of the gimmick, leaving only the rear end uncovered. The positioning of the gimmick and the handkerchiefs is such that you may pick them all up together.

Show the sheet of paper on both sides, roll it into a tube, and secure it with the elastic band. Care should be taken

Fig. 17

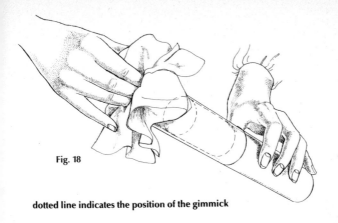

Fig. 18

dotted line indicates the position of the gimmick

to make sure that the tube is of the right size to take the gimmick. It is a good idea to mark the tube beforehand to avoid the chance of mistake.

Pick up the handkerchiefs and gimmick together and, under cover of the handkerchiefs, slip the gimmick into the paper tube (Fig. 18). Start to push both handkerchiefs into the paper tube simultaneously. Then appear to consider for a moment, remove one handkerchief, and push them in one at a time. Before pushing the handkerchiefs through, however, it is a good idea to pass your magic wand quickly behind the paper tube, close up to it so that it appears to be passing right through (Fig. 19), because this gives the

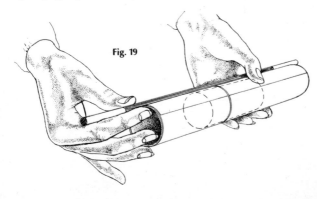

Fig. 19

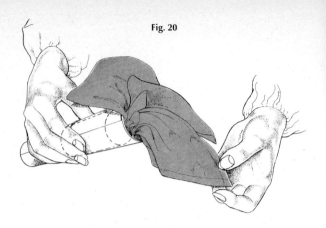

Fig. 20

impression that the tube is empty. If you then push the handkerchiefs one at a time into the tube, using a wand, it will seem, in retrospect, that you have not handled them at all.

Push the handkerchiefs well into the gimmick, and in so doing you will push out first the blue and then the red handkerchief. The way in which the handkerchiefs are removed must be carefully practised. Pull each of them out a little at a time, allowing the edges to fall around the paper tube, and then finally take the handkerchief near its centre and pull it clear, placing it on the table.

When you do this for the red silk, you will of course also remove the gimmick, which is completely concealed because you make sure that the edges of the handkerchief fall over the edges of the paper tube during its removal (Fig. 20). Take care to lay the red handkerchief, with the concealed gimmick, lightly upon the blue silk already on the table to prevent it from talking. Remove the elastic band from the paper tube and show it empty or, if you prefer, tear it into small pieces.

Sweets from a Handkerchief

This is a very popular trick with children. The magician borrows a handkerchief, picks up a plate, and, taking the handkerchief at its centre, gives it a shake, making a shower of sweets fall into the plate.

We have the great French magician, Robert-Houdin, to thank for the invention of the gimmick used in this trick. It consists of a little triangular bag of soft material with a hook-and-ring fastening (Fig. 21). Sweets are placed in the upper bag section, which is closed by bringing up the flap and placing the ring over the wire hook. At the start of the trick, the gimmick either lies on the servante behind your table or in a 'black-art well'. The latter consists of an open hole in the table top with a bag attached directly underneath and made of the same material as the table covering. If black velvet or plush is used and the top is decorated with braid in such a manner that the edges of the pocket, sewn round with braid, appear to be part of the general pattern or design, the hole is invisible even from a very short distance.

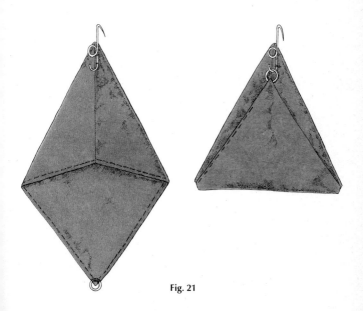

Fig. 21

ROBERT-HOUDIN,

ST. JAMES'S THEATRE.

The celebrated M. ROBERT-HOUDIN will continue his Incredible
Delusions and Extraordinary

FANTASTIQUES

AT THE ABOVE THEATRE,

EVERY

TUESDAY,

THURSDAY,

AND

SATURDAY

EVENINGS,

Doors open at Eight o'clock.

LE FAVORI DES DAMES

A GRAND

DAY

PERFORMANCE

EVERY

WEDNESDAY

MORNING,

Commencing at Half-past Two o'clock.

Houdin's Original Delusions.

*The Programme will comprise a Selection from Robert-Houdin's Original Experiments and
Extraordinary Wonders, in addition to several New and Startling Novelties, including*

THE MIRACULOUS BALANCE,

THE INEXHAUSTIBLE BOTTLE,

SECOND SIGHT,   INVISIBILÉTE,

AND

SUSPENSION ÉTHÉRÉENNE.

BOXES, 4s.　　　PIT, 2s.　　　AMPHITHEATRE, 1s. 6d.

PRIVATE BOXES, ORCHESTRA STALLS, AND TICKETS, MAY BE SECURED AT
MR. MITCHELL'S ROYAL LIBRARY, 33, OLD BOND STREET,
Mr. Sams' Royal Library, St. James's Street; Messrs. Ebers', Hookham's, Allcroft's, Andrews', Leader and Cock's, Chappell's, and Ollivier's Libraries, Bond Street;
Cramer's, and the Carlton Library, 12, Regent Street;
And at the BOX OFFICE of the Theatre, which is open Daily, from Eleven till Five o'clock.

PRINTED BY W. S. JOHNSON, 6, PRINCES STREET, LEICESTER SQUARE.

The borrowed handkerchief is put down on the table to enable you to pick up the plate and show it. When you pick up the handkerchief again, take hold of it at the centre, grasp the wire hook at the top of the gimmick, and secretly bring it under the folds of the handkerchief. A sharp shake is sufficient to unhook the flap and allow the sweets to pour out.

The billiard balls appear, multiply, change colour, and disappear again – by magic!

MAGIC
WITH BALLS

Billiard Balls
Sleight of hand

Many of the sleights described in the section on coin magic are suitable. The palm proper, the finger palm, and the 'De Manche Change' are all adaptable to billiard balls. The positioning of the balls is the same but of course the 'feel' is quite different. Once again practice and more practice is the only way to become expert. Several effects can be achieved either with or without sleight of hand. In most cases, the sleight-of-hand method is 'cleaner' and therefore more effective. Here is such a trick. Which is the better method? First comes an explanation of how the effect can be achieved without sleight of hand.

The magician takes a white billiard ball and wraps it in a sheet of newspaper. The procedure is repeated with a red billiard ball. The wrapped white ball is handed to a spectator to hold but the magician retains the wrapped red ball in full view. On unwrapping the balls, they are seen to have changed places. The spectator now has the red ball, the magician the white.

The secret is simple enough. All you need is a small piece of red glazed paper. Cut two squares of newspaper and glue them together by the edges with the piece of red paper sandwiched between them. In addition, you need an unprepared square of newspaper to match. Wrap the red ball in the unprepared newspaper and the white ball in the faked paper.

In the performance of the trick, when the two balls have been wrapped, you must accidentally mix them up so that it is necessary to check their positions again. To do this, you tear open the newspaper on the white ball, but, revealing the red paper, you claim that it is the red ball. Hand the wrapped red ball to a spectator, who imagines he has the white ball. You hold onto the white ball, which everyone thinks is the red ball. All that is left to do is unwrap the balls, making sure you destroy or at least hide away the prepared sheet of newspaper, and show that the transposition has been accomplished.

Now for the sleight-of-hand version. No special preparation is needed, only an extra white ball. At the start of the trick you have the white ball palmed in your right hand. Pick up the red ball in your right hand and throw a handkerchief over it. Undercover of the handkerchief switch the balls, using the 'De Manche Change' – billiard-ball version, and wrap the white ball in the handkerchief. Give it out directly for a spectator to hold. Now pick up the white ball, throw a second handkerchief over it, and make the switch again, wrapping up the red ball. Immediately hand it out to another spectator. Ditch the white ball into a pocket when convenient. The trick is done, there is nothing to dispose of after the balls are unwrapped, and everything happens in the hands of the audience.

That is why it is worth taking the trouble to learn sleight of hand.

A complete routine

Once you have learned to perform several sleights with balls you will be able to make up your own routine. In other words, you will be able to combine productions, vanishes, colour changes and so on to create an entertaining sequence to last three to five minutes. In the early 1900s Charles Bertram earned an enviable reputation as an expert billiard-ball manipulator. Here is his routine.

First he asked if anyone could lend him a billiard ball. When one was not forthcoming, he proceeded to pinch one, a red one, from the top of his wand. This passed by magic from one hand to the other, appeared from behind his elbow, vanished on being thrown into the air, and was found behind the other elbow. The red ball then multiplied to three, two of which disappeared. The remaining red ball changed to white, which then diminished to half its size. This ball he swallowed, reproducing it from below his chin, and finally vanishing it altogether.

To perform Charles Bertram's routine you will need one large red ball and two red 'shells'. These are hollow half-balls, made of metal or plastic. Also needed are a large white ball, two small white balls, and a small plate.

Place the red ball under the right-hand side of the waistcoat (vest), cummerbund, or belt, depending upon your dress. The two shells, nested together, should be hidden in a similar position on the left side. The large white ball and one small white ball should be in your left coat or trouser pocket, and the remaining small white ball should be in your right waistcoat (vest) or inside coat pocket.

Hold a magic wand in your right hand between your first and second fingers and thumb. Ask if someone can lend you a billiard ball and put your left hand out as though to receive one. This is a neat way of showing your hand empty without calling undue attention to it. At the same time, casually bring your right hand, still holding the wand, to where the red ball is hidden and steal this.

Transfer the wand to your left hand and appear to see a red spot at the top. Remove this with your right hand and reveal the billiard ball. Knock it on the table to prove it solid but explain that it will become soft if you rub it in your hands. Roll the ball between your hands and pretend to place it in your left hand, in reality palming it in your right. This is a billiard-ball version of the 'French Drop'. Turn the back of your left hand to the front, making a rubbing movement (Fig. 1). Then gradually turning it back again, slowly open it and show the hand empty. Reproduce from your right knee. Tap the ball on the table once more to show that it has returned to solidity.

At the same time, however, secretly obtain the two shells from their hiding place on the left. Bring both hands together and slip the shells over the red ball (Fig. 2). Now apparently 'pinch' a second ball from the first by taking off one of the shells and holding it between your right fore-finger and thumb, circling the half shell (Fig. 3). Next swing your hands forward and backwards and, under cover of

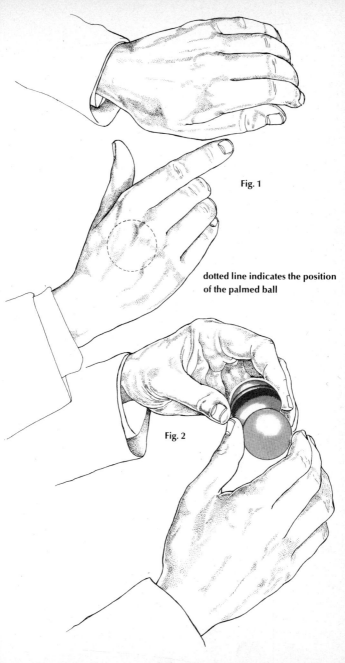

Fig. 1

dotted line indicates the position
of the palmed ball

Fig. 2

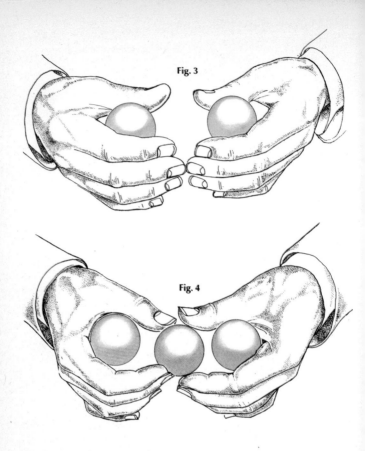

Fig. 3

Fig. 4

this movement, slip the solid ball from the second shell on to your right fingertips. You now have a shell in each hand with the solid ball in the centre, apparently three solid balls (Fig. 4).

Put the shell from your right hand into your left hand and hold it by your fingertips. Let the solid ball roll behind the shells, close your right hand as though holding the missing ball, and appear to swallow it. Now slip the second shell over the first shell and, closing your right hand again as if holding the ball, pretend to throw it to the audience. Under cover of this little diversion, palm off the two shells in your right hand. Turn half right and tap the ball in your left hand on the table, at the same time ditching the shells in your right-hand coat pocket.

Go round the table, making one or two more passes with the solid red ball. Half turn to the left, throw the ball into the air and catch it (Fig. 5). While the eyes of the audience follow the ball's flight, steal the large white ball with your left hand and bring it up quickly to meet your right hand as the red ball falls (Fig. 6). Place the white ball in your right palm (Fig. 7). You are now going to perform the colour change. Take the red ball into your left hand, holding it at the fingertips. Now bring your right hand in front of and over your left hand. Pass your right hand downwards and place the red ball into your right palm with your left fingers, immediately picking up the white ball in its place (Fig. 8). Display the white ball at your left fingertips. Reproduce the red ball from your left elbow and put it down.

A similar set of actions follows to change the large white ball to a small one. Throw the large white ball into the air as misdirection to enable you to steal the small white ball from your left pocket. Make the exchange exactly as described above, so 'turning' the larger white ball to a small one. Then reproduce the large ball from behind your knee and put it down on your table.

Pretend to take the small white ball into your left hand by means of the 'French Drop', in reality palming it in your right hand. Apparently swallow it and reproduce it from the back of your neck. Next actually put the ball in your mouth and pretend to swallow it. Then quite openly remove the second small white ball from your right waist-coat (vest) or inside coat pocket. Once more using the 'French Drop', appear to take this second white ball into your right hand, slap yourself on top of the head, and drop the first small ball out of your mouth. The ball will appear to have passed right through your head and out of your mouth. Ditch the ball palmed in your left hand at your convenience.

This routine will give you a good basis on which to work.

Fig. 5

Fig. 6

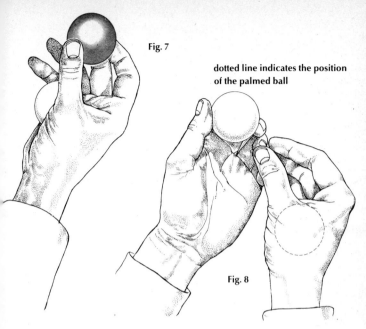

Fig. 7

dotted line indicates the position of the palmed ball

Fig. 8

I think it has one or two drawbacks that could be eliminated. For instance, after the two changes, the colour change, and the diminish, the ball that has 'changed' is immediately reproduced. This proves that only an exchange has taken place, not an actual transfiguration. Secondly, I am not convinced that it is a good thing to start with large balls and end up with a small one. However, I am prepared to be proved wrong and hope that many of my readers will work on the problem.

The Cups and Balls

One of the oldest tricks in the world, 'The Cups and Balls' was first performed by the Hindu fakirs of India and the gully gully men of Egypt centuries ago. They used wooden cups whereas today we use cups of metal. The ancient version was quite crude in performance whereas the Western version has grown into a sophisticated and fascinating combination of sleights, skills, and dodges. Not really suitable for presentation on a big stage, it is, however, a superb effect in a drawing-room or under other close-up conditions.

A number of small balls appear and disappear from under three cups in a bewildering manner. When they should be there, they are not! When they can't possibly be there, they are!

The principle sleights

Palming a ball   The basic palm with these small balls is between the fleshy parts at the bottom of the second and third fingers of your right hand (Fig. 9). The ball is retrieved from this position by your right thumb, which rolls it across your second finger to the tip of the first, where it can be displayed to the audience (Fig. 10). If you keep your thumb in that position, you will be able, by simply reversing the move, to bring the ball straight back into the palm position. Subconsciously you will automatically judge exactly how far the thumb must travel in either direction to perfect the sleight. After much practice you will be able to use this sleight as a vanish, by pretending to place the ball into your left hand from your right fingertips, in reality rolling it with your thumb into the palm position.

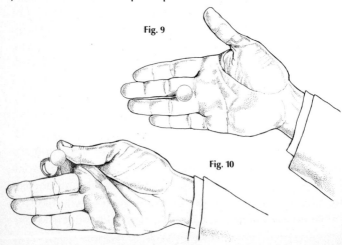

Fig. 9

Fig. 10

Another method of palming This is really the palm proper as already described in the coin magic section. Hold the ball between your forefinger and thumb. Using your thumb, bring the ball to the tips of your third and fourth fingers. Now, by bending these fingers, press the ball into your palm (Fig. 11) and retain it by slight pressure from either side, using the fleshy parts at the base of your palm; then open your fingers (Fig. 12). To reproduce the ball from this position, simply reverse the moves: bend your third and fourth fingers into the palm, roll the ball out of your palm proper more-or-less into the finger palm, where your thumb can reach it, and then roll it to a position between your forefinger and thumb.

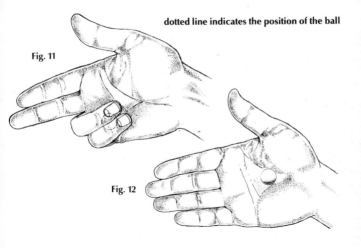

dotted line indicates the position of the ball

Fig. 11

Fig. 12

How to introduce a ball under a cup Normally just before secretly inserting a ball under a cup, it is palmed by one of the methods described. From this palm position you have to roll the ball to between the tip of your forefinger and the ball of your thumb (Fig. 10). Now bend your third and little fingers into your hand until you are able to transfer the ball from its position between your forefinger and thumb to between the top joints of these fingers. Then straighten all your fingers and the ball remains gripped between the

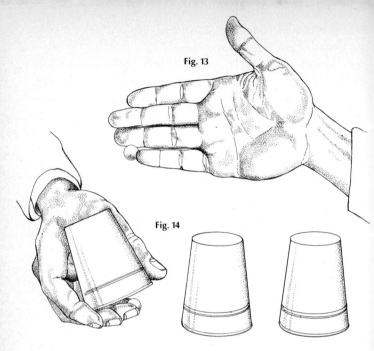

Fig. 13

Fig. 14

third and little fingers (Fig. 13). From this position, it is a very simple matter to introduce the ball when raising a cup (Fig. 14).

A complete routine

The routine I give here is exactly as performed by Charles Bertram, in his day one of England's greatest sleight-of-hand experts.

You will need the three special metal cups, a table napkin which can be borrowed, four small cork balls in your right pocket, three potatoes or tangerines in your left pocket, and a handkerchief, which can also be borrowed. Lay the napkin on your table as a surface to work upon.

Pick up one cup and show it freely. Pick up your wand and measure the cup's depth by putting the wand inside it and 'marking' the edge with your thumb. Then, to 'prove' that it is deeper on the inside than the outside, appear to measure the outside but slide your thumb up the wand to produce the illusion. Take up the second cup, put the wand inside, and tap the bottom two or three times, completely withdrawing the wand each time, to prove it solid. Appear to pass the wand into the cup once more but actually slide it between the cup and your hand so apparently passing right through the bottom of the cup.

An old German engraving of a typical street magician. On his table are the elements of his art: cups of varying sizes, a pack of cards, dice, coins, and a wand.

Next you appear to pass one cup right through another. Pick up a cup in each hand at their brims. Drop the cup in your right hand into the cup in your left hand. Immediately release the cup from your left hand and catch instead the dropped cup. Finally catch the cup that has been released from your left hand in your right hand. The whole move is the work of a moment. A little practice in front of a mirror will show you how effective the illusion can be. All three cups may then be handed out for examination.

While this is being done, steal and palm one ball from your right-hand pocket. Produce this ball from the tip of the wand, appear to place it in your left hand but in fact retain it, palmed between the second and third fingers of your right hand.

Now arrange the three cups in a row on the napkin. Tilt the left-hand cup with your right hand and apparently pass the ball from your left hand underneath it (Fig. 15). Produce a second ball from the tip of your wand, actually the first ball that was palmed in your right hand. Pretend to place this under the centre cup, actually palming it again. For a third time apparently produce a ball from the wand and really place this under the third cup.

However, as you do so, pretend to steal it away again. Make out you hear someone query this move, tilt the third cup, and show the ball actually underneath. Pick up the ball in your right hand, apparently place it in your left hand, but actually retain it palmed in your right. Appear to place the ball under the third cup once again with your left hand – which is in fact empty.

Now you say that there is a ball under each cup, but that you will remove each of them in turn by magic. Tap the

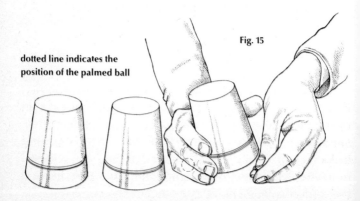

dotted line indicates the position of the palmed ball

Fig. 15

left-hand cup with your wand and produce the ball palmed in your right hand from its tip. Show the cup empty. Appear to pass this ball into your wand by apparently placing the ball in your left hand, actually palming it in the right, and passing your wand right through your closed left hand, afterwards showing it empty.

Next produce a 'second' ball by 'pinching' it from the top of the centre cup and showing the cup empty. Appear to put this ball into your left hand and then make it disappear into the wand. Apparently catch the third ball above the right-hand cup and show this cup empty. Place the ball on the table to the left and secretly obtain a second ball in your right hand. Pick up the visible ball from the table with your left hand, appear to pinch a piece from it, and show the second ball in your right hand. An effective 'bit' here is to click one fingernail against another as the second ball is pinched off.

Place both balls on the table and show all three cups empty. Pick up the balls, one in each hand, and apparently transfer the ball in your right hand to your left hand, actually palming it. Lift the centre cup with your right hand and appear to place both balls from your left hand underneath, actually of course only one moves. Show the outside cups empty, and then secretly introduce the palmed ball under the right-hand cup.

You now say that you will pass one of the balls under the centre cup to each of the outside cups. Tap the centre cup with your wand, appear to remove a ball from its tip, and toss this imaginary ball into the air. Raise the centre cup and show only one ball to be there. Pick up this ball and apparently place it in your left hand and return it under the cup. Actually you have it palmed in your right hand. Pick up the left-hand cup but the ball has not arrived there. Secretly introduce the palmed ball. Then lift up the right-hand cup and show the ball there. Now touch the centre cup with your wand and pretend to pick a ball from the end and pass it through the base of the left-hand cup.

Lift this left-hand cup and show the ball to your audience.

You now have two balls on the table, one in front of each of the two outside cups. Steal the two balls remaining in your right pocket. Ask your audience which one of the visible balls is the larger. It does not matter which is chosen. You pick up the chosen ball and appear to break a piece off which becomes a third ball. Actually, of course, it is the first of the palmed balls and you still retain one ball palmed in your right hand.

Place the two visible balls down on the table to join the third and show the three cups empty, introducing the palmed ball under the right-hand cup. Pick up one ball and apparently place it under the centre cup but actually palm it. Pick up a second ball and place it under the left-hand cup, together with the palmed ball. Pick up the third ball, pretend to place it in your left hand, and actually palm it in your right. Take up your wand and tap your left hand, show it empty, and say that the third ball has passed under the right-hand cup. Prove this point by tipping up the right-hand cup and showing the ball there, but secretly also introduce the ball palmed in your right hand as you replace the cup on the table.

Pretend to extract the ball magically from the centre cup and offer to pass it under either of the other two cups. It doesn't matter which cup is chosen as they both conceal two balls. Pick up the chosen cup, show the two balls, and pick these up one in each hand. Pretend to return them both, actually replacing only one and palming the other.

Say that they have chosen the correct cup but, had they chosen the other, you could take one of the balls just shown and make it magically pass over. So saying, produce the palmed ball from the end of your wand. Apparently place the ball in your left hand, actually palming it, and appear to throw it towards the other outside cup. Lift and show two balls and, in replacing the cup, introduce the palmed ball, making three in all. Lift the originally chosen cup and show only one ball. Pick this up to emphasize the point and then, in apparently returning it, actually palm the ball. Touch this cup with the wand and command the ball to pass to the other outside cup. Lift this and show the three balls.

Ask someone up to assist you. Place the three visible balls, one in front of each cup, and borrow a handkerchief. Take the four corners of the handkerchief between the thumb and forefinger of your left hand to make a 'bag'. Ask the spectator to examine the cups and place a ball under each.

Next you ask how many balls he or she would like you to produce. Say the answer is twelve. Give the spectator the wand and ask that each cup be touched in turn. Each time a cup is touched, lift it up, and remove the ball, introducing the palmed ball as it is set down again. Pretend to drop the visible ball into the handkerchief, actually palming it. Raise the next cup that is tapped, remove the ball, and secretly introduce the palmed ball. Again, apparently place the ball in the handkerchief but actually palm it. Continue like this until the correct number of balls has been produced.

Give the handkerchief, as though containing the balls, to the spectator to hold. Count three and snatch the handkerchief away: the balls have vanished. You say that the balls have simply returned to the cups and, under the misdirection of picking up the cup on the left with your right hand to show the ball underneath, steal a small potato or tangerine with your left hand. Immediately cover this with the cup and return the cup to the table with the potato or whatever is underneath it.

Repeat this move with the other two cups until you have three cups on the table with a potato underneath each and a ball in front of each. Pick up each ball in turn, apparently place it in your left hand while actually retaining it in your right, and pretend to pass it magically under the appropriate cup. Ask the spectator to raise the cups and you can imagine the surprise when three potatoes are discovered.

MAGIC
WITH THIMBLES

The principle moves

First move   The thimble is placed on the right forefinger, and the left hand begins to close round it, apparently to draw it off (Fig. 1). Under cover of the left hand, the right forefinger is actually bent inwards (Fig. 2) and the thimble is thumb palmed in the right hand. The right forefinger is immediately extended again and the left hand completes its closing action and is then drawn away, leaving the right forefinger pointing towards it to increase the misdirection (Fig. 3).

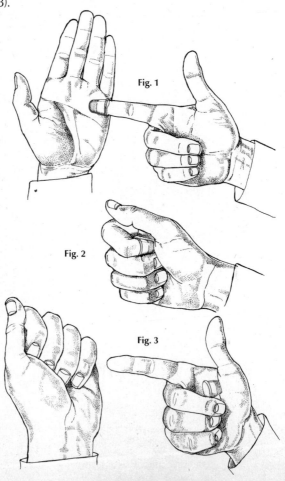

Fig. 1

Fig. 2

Fig. 3

Second move   The thimble is on the right forefinger. The left hand is formed into a fist and the thimble finger is pushed into it (Fig. 4). The right forefinger is bent round the left thumb (Fig. 5) and leaves the thimble thumb palmed in the right hand as before. The right forefinger is withdrawn and the left hand moves away, leaving the right forefinger still extended (Fig. 6).

It is important to note that the left hand moves away from the right in each case because by moving the right hand away from the left the illusion is greatly diminished.

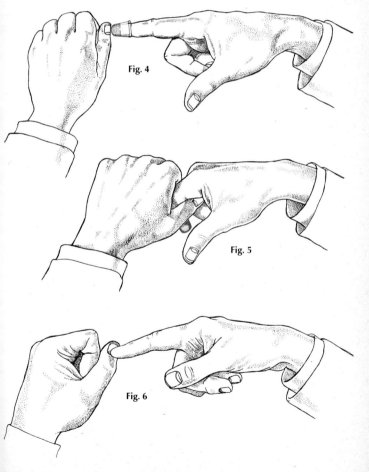

Fig. 4

Fig. 5

Fig. 6

Third move   The thimble is on the right forefinger, which is placed slowly in the mouth, withdrawn, and then replaced quickly, but by bending the finger, thumb-palming the thimble, and instantly extending it again, only the finger goes into the mouth the second time. The thimble is apparently swallowed and produced elsewhere.

Fourth move   The thimble is placed on the right forefinger and exhibited behind the left hand (Fig. 7). Repeat this movement, but in doing so, and while the right hand is passing up behind the left, the thimble is transferred from the first to the second finger by gripping it between the third finger and the thumb, withdrawing the first finger, and inserting the second (Fig. 8). The left hand now apparently closes round the thimble and draws it off, but the second finger of the right hand is actually bent down still bearing the thimble and the empty forefinger is extended into the left hand (Fig. 9).

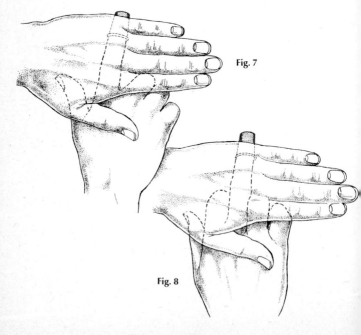

Fig. 7

Fig. 8

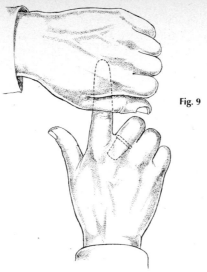

Fig. 9

Fifth move　The change-over palm can be executed with a thimble to show both hands empty, back and front. The thimble is palmed (not thumb palmed) in the right hand, the forefinger of which points towards the left while that hand is being shown back and front (Fig. 10). This is done while standing slightly towards the left and then a turn is made towards the right in order to show the other hand in the same way.

　As the hands pass each other with a sweeping movement, the second or third finger of the left hand is bent inwards and 'hooked' into the thimble at the moment of contact (Fig. 11). The right hand can then be shown while the left

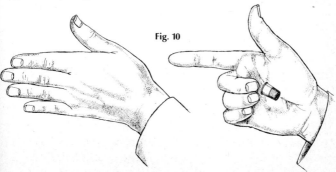

Fig. 10

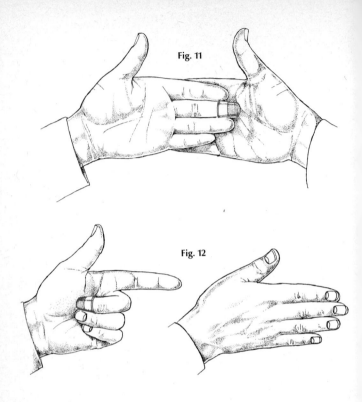

Fig. 11

Fig. 12

forefinger points to it quite naturally (Fig. 12). The entire movement can be repeated if desired because in the return sweep of the hands the thimble can be easily left palmed in the right hand, its original position.

Sixth move A thimble can be quite easily vanished or produced by means of the back-hand palm. Gripped between the first and third fingers, it can be vanished by slightly bending the second finger downwards and backwards so that the thimble revolves into a position behind this finger (Fig. 13). To reproduce, bend the second finger downwards and slightly backwards again, thus revolving the thimble into an upright position ready to receive the finger.

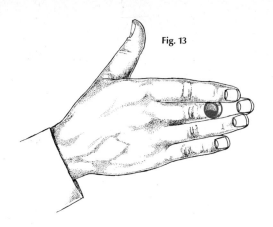

Fig. 13

A complete routine

A red-white-and-blue thimble multiplies into three – one red, one white, and one blue. The red one is vanished and reproduced several times, eventually multiplying into ten. The white one also multiplies, but into five, and likewise the blue. The thimbles are all vanished, and incidentally the spectators, believing they know where they have really gone, are 'sold again'.

In this routine devised by Ivor C. Smith, you will need a table fitted with a black-art well or any other type of table trap. The former is preferred, owing to its simplicity. Your other equipment comprises one lemon, one paper bag, one red-white-and-blue thimble, fourteen red thimbles, eight white thimbles, eight blue thimbles, and five holders for thimbles. These are standard metal holders obtainable from most magic-dealers and consist of small metal plates with elastic loops to hold the thimbles in position so that they can be easily and quickly obtained on the fingers when required (Fig. 14). One edge of the plate is bent over at right angles to form a ledge on which the ends of the thimbles can rest. A pin secures the plate in position.

It will perhaps be as well to state here that holders of the

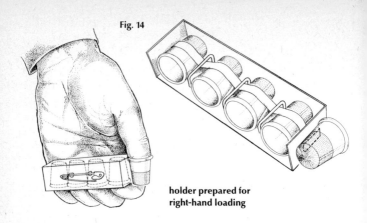

Fig. 14

holder prepared for right-hand loading

usual stock pattern take only four thimbles, whereas three of those mentioned below, Holders A, D, and E, are to be loaded with five each. If this is not done, it means sacrificing the production on the thumbs, and in my opinion failure to do this ruins the whole effect. There are several sleight-of-hand methods for overcoming the difficulty, but they need not be considered here as it is a perfectly easy matter to attach the fifth thimble to each of these holders in such a position that it can be simply and quickly obtained on the thumb. As the exact position varies a good deal according to the size and shape of the hand, it is impossible to lay down a hard and fast rule. (Figure 14 shows my own method of loading the left hand from Holder A.)

The thimbles are previously placed in position as follows. Holder A, loaded with five red thimbles, is placed on the left trouser leg and hidden by the coat or in a tiered or pocketed skirt. Holder B, loaded with four white thimbles, is placed under the front edge of a waistcoat (vest) or under a belt. Holder C, loaded with four blue thimbles, is fastened in a similar position but on the right side.

Holder D is loaded with thimbles in the following order – red, white, blue, white, red – so that, when they are obtained and exhibited on the right hand, a red thimble will appear on the little finger and also on the thumb, the blue thimble on the middle or second finger, and a white thimble on each of the two remaining fingers, namely the first and third. This holder is fastened into the top inside breast pocket on the left side.

The remaining holder, E, is loaded with thimbles in the order red, blue, white, blue, red, and these will eventually be produced on the left hand. They are placed either in the left trouser pocket (if wearing evening dress) or in the left-side coat pocket. The lemon, in the latter case, is placed in the coat pocket on the opposite side, but in the case of evening dress the right trouser pocket is really the only alternative.

Make three holes in the side of a matchbox, cardcase, or similar article, and place three of the remaining thimbles (one red, one white, and one blue) in the holes, which should be large enough to allow the thimbles to go nearly but not quite into the box. The four remaining red thimbles, W, X, Y, and Z, are disposed of as follows. Thimble W is placed in the right shoe; Thimble X in the left shoe. Thimble Y is placed in the collar on the right side; Thimble Z in the collar on the left side. This will leave only the tricolour thimble, which may be either on the table or magically produced to commence the trick.

After exhibiting this thimble on the left forefinger, take up the wand from the table with the right hand and 'mesmerize' the thimble with it. In replacing the wand on the table, carelessly move the matchbox, card-case, or similar article used, and at the same time obtain possession of the three thimbles concealed therein on the second, third, and fourth fingers of the right hand.

Remove the tricolour thimble and place it on the right forefinger, keeping the other fingers closed to conceal those just obtained. Apparently place the thimble in the left hand, really thumb-palming it in the right (i.e. holding it in the fork of the thumb and forefinger as shown in Figure 3). Slowly open the left hand, simultaneously making an upward movement as if throwing the thimble into the air.

Reach out in the same direction with the right hand and immediately extend the fingers, disclosing the three thimbles.

Take these off one at a time with the left hand and place them on the table just in front of the black-art well. In taking off the red one with the forefinger and thumb, place the third finger of left hand into the tricolour thimble, which is still thumb palmed in the right hand, and carry it away to drop into the black-art well in the act of placing the other thimble on the table.

Take up the red thimble and proceed to make various passes with it as may be desired until a point at which it is apparently taken in the left hand but really thumb palmed in the right. Vanish from the left hand, and then produce Thimble X from the left shoe on the first finger of the left hand.

While doing this, the thimble retained in the right hand is transferred to the fourth or little finger of that hand, and this, for some performers, is the most difficult move of the whole trick, depending to a great extent on the size and shape of the hand. It is for this reason that Thimble X is produced from the left shoe; bending down to obtain it greatly assists in covering any awkward movement – in fact, the right hand can even be pressed against the body if necessary so that the operation becomes a much simpler matter.

Thimble X is then placed on the right forefinger and again apparently transferred to the left hand, but once more thumb palmed in the right. Vanish as before and produce Thimble Y from the right side of the collar on the left forefinger, meanwhile getting the third finger of the right hand into Thimble X.

Transferring Thimble Y to the right forefinger, repeat the previous vanish, this time producing Thimble W from the right shoe and getting Y on the second finger of the right hand. The next and last pass will produce Thimble Z from the left side of the collar, but Thimble W is retained thumb palmed in the right hand, which is now brought up in front of the body with the back of the hand towards the audience and the fingers closed sufficiently to conceal the thimbles.

Place Thimble Z on the right thumb, which is extended upwards, and patter as to the curious effect caused by doing this. Close the forefinger into Thimble W, which is in the exact position to receive it, and raise the right hand slowly upwards toward the left side, meanwhile loading the left hand with five red thimbles from Holder A on the left-hand trouser or from the skirt.

Produce and exhibit all ten red thimbles. Take them off one at a time and place them in front of the black-art well on the table. Then, standing on the right-hand side of the table, take up the blue thimble, and place it on the right thumb. This must be done without the assistance of the left hand, which meanwhile obtains possession of the four white thimbles from Holder B on the left side of the waistcoat (vest) or belt.

Extend the left arm, the back of the hand towards the audience with the fingers closed and the thumb pointing downwards, and place the white thimble from the table on the left thumb with the right hand. Bring the left hand slowly down without bending the arm, and continue in a circular movement across the body in front of the knees and upwards on the right side, at the same time making a turn towards the right and getting the four blue thimbles from Holder C onto the fingers of the right hand.

As the left hand arrives at its highest point on the right side, extend the fingers and exhibit the thimbles. Immediately stretch out the right hand (with only the blue thimble on the thumb exposed) to the same position and sweep it back in the same manner to the left side. Extend the fingers and exhibit the blue thimbles.

Take all the thimbles off and place them with the red ones in front of the black-art well on the table.

The next step is to exhibit an empty paper bag, and, having shown this to be genuine, take up the thimbles a handful at a time and apparently place them in the bag. Now for the little swindle. The thimbles, of course, really go into the well in the act of sweeping them up, but there is no reason why one or two may not be actually taken up in the hand and partially exposed in carrying them towards the bag. These, of course, are not dropped into the bag but are carried back again and eventually go into the well with the others. Before placing the hand apparently containing thimbles into the bag, however, a slightly suspicious movement is made in the direction of the pocket containing the lemon, and this is repeated on each occasion before thimbles are supposedly added.

The bag is then blown out and 'popped' in the approved fashion, between the hands, showing that the thimbles have vanished. The remains of the bag are rolled up and tossed to the audience. Now, if the above moves have been followed correctly, the audience will be quite sure that the thimbles are really in your pocket.

Offer to explain the trick and state that, strange though it may seem, the answer to the whole trick is contained 'in there', indicating the pocket where the spectators really believe the thimbles to be. Request a member of the audience to place a hand in the pocket and bring out any thimbles found there.

'Of course,' you say, 'I don't want you to go interfering with any of my personal belongings which may be there, but merely to bring out the thimbles.'

Naturally the volunteer will state that there are no thimbles there.

'No thimbles? Well, I stated that the answer to the trick was in that pocket, so will you please turn the pocket inside out and bring out anything that is there.'

Out comes the lemon.

'Quite correct. The answer is a lemon. And, by the way, don't let this worry you at all because there are the thimbles.'

At the same time exhibit both hands, the fingers and

thumbs of each being capped with coloured thimbles.

The last move, although perhaps the best, is quite the simplest. As your assistant is about to feel in your pocket, it is quite natural that you should turn that side slightly towards the front so that everyone may see what is being done, and this gives an easy opportunity to obtain the thimbles from Holder E on the left-hand side. It is also quite natural that you should raise your right arm, bent at the elbow, so that the assistant has freer access to your pocket. This will incidentally bring your right hand very near the left inside breast pocket and the thimbles are easily obtained from Holder D, which is fastened there.

That, then, is the little thimble sequence which I have frequently used, and which is undoubtedly a winner every time. On the other hand, there is no reason at all why it should not be very much enlarged if desired.

When you realize that clips of thimbles can be attached to the table, chair backs, pieces of apparatus, trays, in fact almost anything, there is practically no limit to the production. Another idea would be to construct tiny black-art wells or troughs in the table top, just deep enough to contain a clip or single thimbles yet bringing their edges level with the top. If this were done, the very act of resting the hand on the table, or even of putting other thimbles down, would suffice to get a full load again.

From two small metal rings comes a mass of brightly coloured paper ribbon – and a rabbit!

PAPER MAGIC

Snowstorm in China

This is one of the prettiest effects in the whole realm of magic. It far transcends the simplicity of the method.

The magician takes one or two pieces of tissue paper, dips them into a tumbler of water, and makes them into a wet 'blob'. The paper is squeezed and shaken to remove excess water, placed in the left hand, and fanned. Suddenly, tiny pieces of paper, like confetti, start to emerge from the closed left fist. The more the magician fans, the more confetti appears, until there is a veritable snowstorm.

You will need a fan, a tumbler of water, some confetti, and several sheets of tissue paper. The only preparation is the making of a little confetti parcel. Just wrap a small amount of it in a piece of tissue paper, screw up one end of the parcel, and use this end to attach it between two folds of the closed fan near the handle.

Begin with the fan in your right hand. Then pass it to your obviously empty left hand and pick up the pieces of tissue in your right. Dip them into the water, squeeze them into a ball, and shake off the surplus water. You are now apparently going to place the wet tissue in your 'empty' left hand, so you must at the same time take the fan back into your right hand. Actually what happens is you pretend to put the wet tissue in your left hand but retain it in your right instead, bringing the confetti parcel into view as if it were wet tissue and taking the fan in your right hand.

All you have to do now is squeeze the parcel in your left hand to break the tissue and allow the confetti to emerge, wafted into the air by the fan. At the height of the storm, allow the outer tissue of the confetti parcel, screwed up as small as possible, to drop unnoticed on the floor. When all the confetti has gone, you can show your left hand empty.

Although this is a simple trick, or perhaps, because this is a simple trick, it requires much practice. When you have practised the switch a few dozen times in front of a mirror, it will become second nature. A trick of this beauty demands that of you.

Many magicians will use multi-coloured confetti for this effect because it is so much easier to obtain. However, if you had ever seen it done with snow-white paper as I have, you would accept nothing else.

Silks from Tissue

The magician shows three strips of tissue paper, red, white, and blue. They are set alight in the flame of a candle and allowed to burn to ashes. When the ashes are rubbed together, the audience is amazed to see the same colours appear – red, white, and blue – but not tissue strips this time, real silk ribbon, lots of it. But it doesn't end there because the ribbons gradually blend together and are transformed into the Stars and Stripes, the Union Jack, or some other appropriate national flag.

You will need about 13 feet (4 m) each of red, white, and blue ribbon. Stitch these together at one end and stitch that end to a small piece of material to match your clothing, preferably black. Roll the ribbons up from the loose ends and cover the bundle with the cloth. Hide this bundle under your left arm near the top. Bunch up the national flag and hide it under your trouser waistband or belt on the left-hand side, almost on your hip.

Pick up the tissue strips, screw them up, and set them alight by holding them in the flame of the candle. This screwing up is a good move because it makes the tissues burn more slowly and they are therefore more manageable. As the tissues are burning, show your hands one at a time to be empty, passing the paper from one hand to the other. Next you show that there is nothing up your sleeves. Draw up your right sleeve with your left hand. Pass the burning paper to your left hand, pull up your left sleeve with your right hand, and at the same time steal the ribbon bundle from under your left arm.

Immediately squash up the papers between both hands, get hold of the cloth covering in your right hand, and with a forceful throw unfold the ribbons so that they shoot forward towards your audience. At the same time grab the flag with your left hand and bring it quickly to the ribbons. Being of the same colours, it will not be noticed. Gather up the ribbons in short lengths, bring them behind the flag, and then suddenly open it up, keeping the ribbons well concealed behind it.

Torn and Restored Paper

There are numerous variations of the torn and restored paper trick. Some perform it with a long strip of tissue paper; some with newspaper. Sometimes it is performed with specially printed sheets of paper appropriate to a funny patter story. Here I provide you with an explanation of the basic trick.

The magician shows a small strip of tissue paper and proceeds to tear it into several pieces. These are crushed into a small ball and both hands are shown empty. Then the ball is unrolled and the strip of paper is seen to be whole once more.

At the beginning of the trick you conceal a second, balled-up, whole piece of tissue nipped between your first and second fingers. Pick up the first strip of tissue and tear it down the middle. Put the two pieces together and tear them down the middle again. Repeat this until the pieces are quite small. Then roll them into a ball. Take this ball in your right hand at the fingertips and, at the same time, roll the balled-up second tissue behind it with your thumb. Show the two balls of paper as one, which will give you the opportunity to demonstrate that both hands are otherwise empty. Open out the whole strip to show the tissue restored, concealing the balled-up pieces between your first and second fingers. Screw the lot together into a ball, toss it aside, and get on with the next trick.

The Sun and Moon

The magician shows two small squares of tissue paper, one red and one white, and cuts circles out of the centres of each of them. All the pieces of tissue are then screwed up together and set alight. From the ashes the magician produces the tissues restored, but there has been a mistake. The red tissue has a white centre and the white tissue a red centre! The papers are squashed up once more and given to a spectator to hold. After a wave of the magic wand, the tissues are opened up and found to be perfectly restored, the centres having returned to their proper, or in other words original, places.

You will need to prepare two of the papers beforehand by cutting out central circles and gluing in the contrasting centres. Place these two prepared sheets together, squash them into a ball, and hide it in your waistband or under your waistcoat (vest) on the left side of your body. Take one ordinary red sheet and one ordinary white sheet, roll them together, and hide them on the right side of your body. Put one sheet of each colour on your table, together with some scissors and a candle.

Ask a member of your audience to help by cutting the circles from the squares of tissue. To ensure that the circles are of the correct size, previously fold each of the tissues into four and mark where it has to be cut with a pencil. Direct the spectator to cut around the pencil mark but do not draw the attention of the rest of your audience to this part of the action.

Walk forward and show the sheets, making it very obvious that the centres have been cut out. Then roll the pieces into a ball and, as you return to your table, steal the prepared sheets with your left hand. Set light to the original sheets and, when they are almost reduced to ashes, bring your left hand to join your right hand, putting out the flames as you do so.

Part your hands, showing that the tissues are restored. Open up the sheets and reveal that they have the wrong centres. Show them first to the left, and then, as you make a half turn to the right to show them that side, steal the balled-up sheets from their hiding place on the right-hand side of your body. Crumple the incorrect sheets into a ball and, using the 'De Manche Change', switch the ordinary tissues for the incorrect ones.

Give the balled-up ordinary tissues to someone to hold while you get your wand. If you like, you can ditch the palmed incorrect sheets at this point or you can do it at the end. Wave the wand over the spectator's hand and ask that the bundle be opened. When it is, the centres are shown to be restored to their correct tissues.

The Japanese Butterflies

This makes a very pleasant interlude in an act, especially if performed in Japanese or Chinese costume.

Two butterflies are fashioned out of pieces of ordinary tissue paper. The magician fans them with a Japanese fan and they flutter about the stage as though they have come to life. They can settle and rise again, all under the control of the performer. They really do appear to have become live butterflies.

The secret is a length of silk thread. Tie the thread at its centre to the top button of your coat, or waistcoat (vest) if worn. Have a small pellet of wax fixed to each end. Tear out the butterfly shapes, twist them in the middle, and bend up their wings a little. Secretly attach one end of the thread to each butterfly by means of the wax pellets.

Place the butterflies on your flat left hand and begin to fan them rapidly. Once you have managed to get them into the air, gentle waves of the fan along the direction of the threads will keep them flying. It is important that the current of air produced by the fan be directed along the thread and not from above or below.

If you wish the butterflies to settle, simply reduce the 'fanning power' and thereby cut down on the air pressure. To get them started again, you must begin fanning very vigorously. As is so often the case, despite the simplicity of the idea, this item requires a lot of practice in order to achieve the standard of performance it deserves.

The Famous Afghan Bands

It is said that this was originally performed in the East, using turban cloth. The magician shows three strips of paper, each of which has been glued together at the ends to form a ring. Using a pair of scissors, one ring is cut down the centre lengthwise. The result is of course two rings, half as wide but otherwise the same size. A second ring is treated in exactly the same way but this time it becomes one large ring, half as wide but twice as long. Finally the third ring is cut, again lengthwise, and this time to the audience's utter amazement it turns into two rings as in the first instance but they are linked together!

Although extremely effective, the secret is simplicity itself. In forming the rings, glue the ends of the first one together quite normally. But, before joining the ends of the second ring, give the paper a single twist, and, before joining the ends of the third ring, give it two twists (Fig. 1).

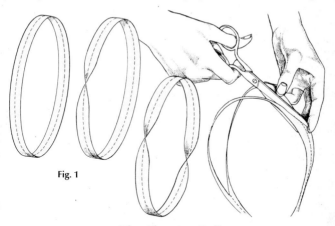

Fig. 1

The Floating Ball

A sheet of tissue paper is rolled into a ball and dropped onto the stage. The magician makes mysterious passes over the ball and it rises into the air. Then a small hoop is taken and passed over the ball to prove that it is not held by threads or other natural means. Finally the tissue is opened up and thrown into the audience for examination.

Probably the most successful way of performing this great effect is upon a stage with the help of at least one off-stage assistant. A very fine silk thread is stretched across the stage and either held by two assistants, one either side, or fixed at one side and held by an assistant at the other. The thread passes over a table and through the small hoop, which rests on the table. In rolling the paper into a ball, you in fact wrap it around the thread. By manipulating the thread, the assistant or assistants can cause the ball to rise and move through the air at will. It is also a simple matter to pass the hoop over the ball without its being impeded by the thread as it runs through the hoop.

A one-man version of 'The Float' can be performed as follows. Fix one end of the thread to a table and a small button to the free end. Coil the thread neatly on the table and position the button near the hoop. Pick up the hoop, together with the button, and walk away from the table until the thread is almost taut. Put the hoop over your head and secretly pop the button into your mouth. Make the ball around the thread as before. You are now able to control the movements of the ball by walking about the stage, bending forward, and by hooking the thread over your thumbs and gesturing with your hands. You are also able to pass the hoop over the ball and back over your head again. At the end, take the ball into both hands, open it up, thus releasing it from the thread, and show it to be unprepared. Dispose of the button and thread as you replace the hoop on the table.

The Paddle Trick

No book on magic for students would be complete without a trick using the 'Paddle Move'. Hundreds of different versions of this trick have been invented over the years and every magic-dealer stocks at least two or three variations. This is the original method, the basis of all others.

Six tiny scraps of paper are moistened and stuck to the blade of an ordinary table knife, three on each side. The performer, with forefinger at the rear and thumb on top, removes two pieces at the same time and shows that now only two pieces remain on each side. Another two are removed, one from each side, and the remaining one left on each side is shown. These are removed and the knife blade is completely empty. Then, with a quick flick three pieces suddenly return to one side and, when the blade is turned over, three pieces are seen on that side too!

As already hinted, the secret of this trick lies in what is called the 'Paddle Move'. To facilitate the move, it is best if the knife handle is square, with four distinct flat sides.

Tear a piece of paper into six, trying to match the pieces. Dip them in water and stick them on the blade. Hold the knife in your right hand with the wrist facing upwards and the blade pointing downwards and apparently remove the uppermost pieces, one either side of the blade, between your left forefinger and thumb. Actually you remove only the front piece and dispose of it. Now you are going to turn the knife over to show that both sides hold only two pieces each, but we know that the reverse side still has three pieces, so we must fool the audience by means of the 'Paddle Move'.

Fig. 2

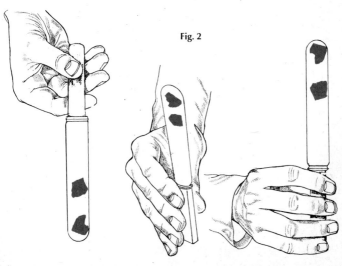

185

By making a full turn of the knife instead of only a half turn, you in fact show the same side twice. To do this, hold the knife as shown and turn your hand inwards towards yourself at the wrist to bring the back of your hand towards the audience, but at the same time rotate the knife between your fingers and thumb so that they 'change sides' on the handle (Fig. 2). So, although the turn of your hand should bring the reverse side of the knife to the front, the simultaneous action of the fingers rotating the knife nullifies the move, bringing the same side to the front again. I have explained this action at some length because it is a very useful dodge to know. As you progress, you will find it used in several quite different effects.

Back to the table knife. You have just apparently shown that two pieces of paper have been removed and therefore only two pieces remain on each side. Reverse the 'Paddle Move' to bring the knife back to its original position and apparently remove two more pieces. Show what appears to be only one piece on each side. Apparently remove the last two pieces and now show the knife seemingly quite empty on both sides. A quick half-turn will reverse the knife and reveal three of the pieces; the 'Paddle Move' will show three pieces on each side. Remove 'all' the pieces by running your left forefinger and thumb down either side of the blade and the trick is complete.

The Tambourine Trick

Two metal rings are shown and, by pressing a sheet of stiff white paper between them, the magician creates a tambourine. But this is a magic tambourine because, when a hole is made at the centre of the paper, out gushes a seemingly endless stream of coloured paper ribbon. This forms a mound of twisted paper, from which the magician produces a large white rabbit.

You will need two metal rings of such a size that, when one is pressed within the other with a sheet of paper between them, the paper is held fast and taut like a drum skin. In addition to the rings and paper, you will require the paper ribbon known by the magic-dealers as a 'tambourine coil', a pair of scissors, and of course a white rabbit! (Or any alternative item which you might prefer to use for the final production.)

Unknown to your audience, the coil is hidden on your table, slightly jutting out over the back edge. It cannot be seen because you cover it with a table cloth, making sure, by folding the cloth back over the coil, that it does not impede the coil's removal. The rabbit (or whatever) is hidden on a chair servante.

Pick up the rings from the table and show how they rest one within the other. Then take up the sheet of paper and show it on both sides (Fig. 3). Put one ring on the table, place the paper over it, and form the tambourine by positioning the second ring on top and pressing the rings together, thus trapping the paper inside them. Show both sides of the tambourine and then put it down on the table again as you pick up the scissors. The second time you take up the tambourine, pick up the coil with it (Fig. 4). The surplus paper will help you to hide this move. Now, with the coil secretly pressed into the tambourine at the back, trim off that surplus.

Take your magic wand, tap a hole in the centre of the paper (Fig. 5), and begin producing the ribbon. With your wand, catch the end of the ribbon, make a fast circular motion, and the paper will spin around the wand and stream out of the tambourine at great speed (Fig. 6). This is a very pretty and even exciting effect.

When the coil is finally exhausted, allow the twisted ribbon to fall upon the chair (Fig. 7). Then bundle up the ribbon in your left hand, and, as you raise it from the chair, steal the load with your right hand and bring it up behind the ribbon unknown to the audience. Walk forward and hold out the ribbon for your applause. Then, just as it is beginning to wane, reach into the paper and produce the rabbit (Fig. 8).

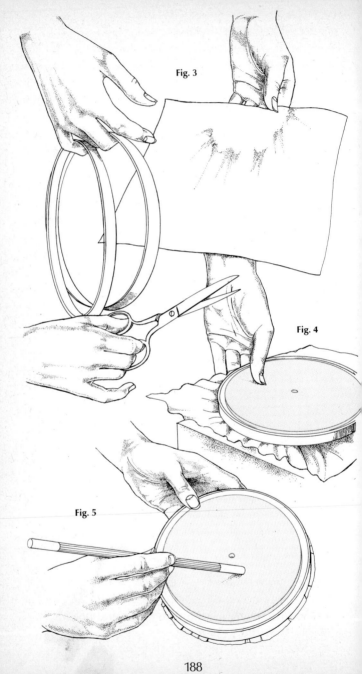

Fig. 3

Fig. 4

Fig. 5

Fig. 6

Fig. 7

Fig. 8

Paper to Sweets

Having produced a huge quantity of brightly coloured paper ribbons when you perform 'The Tambourine Trick', it seems a shame simply to throw them away. Here is a trick which puts them to good use.

The magician comes forward with a large box filled with a jumble of different coloured paper ribbons. Next he or she forms a cone with a square of paper and proceeds to fill it with the ribbon. Once filled, the magician waves magic hands over the top, breaks open the cone at its point, and out flows a large quantity of sweets, much to the delight of the children in the audience.

There are two cones. At the start of the trick, a second, smaller cone, filled with sweets, lies concealed under the paper ribbon in the box. You make the larger cone in full view and, in order to fill it with paper ribbons, dip it into the box. Once out of sight, you quickly load in the smaller cone complete with sweets and bring the larger cone out again with a few bits of ribbon on top. Simply tear off the lower end of the larger cone, at the same time tearing off the lower end of the smaller cone as well, and the sweets will pour out. Catch them on a plate and pass them around.

The Indian Ribbons

Once more we can make use of the coloured paper ribbon left over from some production effect. This time it is a dry version of the fabulous 'The Indian Sands Trick' explained on page 206.

The magician shows three plates, each containing a bundle of ribbon and each bundle of a different colour. The bundles are dropped into a previously shown empty box and mixed together so that they become a jumbled mass of different colours. The audience calls out the colours in turn, and on each request the magician reaches into the box and produces a handful of ribbon of the selected colour and fills the appropriate plate.

As in 'The Sands of India', you need a 'load', or secretly

introduced bundle, for each of the colours. These are simply made by preparing a parcel of each colour and keeping each one intact by gluing a band of matching coloured tissue around it. Underneath the plate containing the red ribbon, hide the red parcel. Underneath the blue plate, the blue parcel, and the same again for yellow.

Show the box empty and then, as you tip the contents of your plates into it, also drop in the secret parcels. When a colour is called, simply bring out the appropriate parcel. Break open the tissue and produce the ribbon. The tissue will not be spotted amongst the ribbon when it is put on its plate.

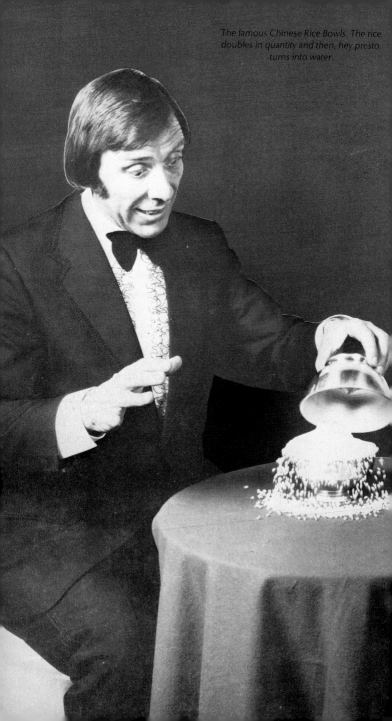

The famous Chinese Rice Bowls. The rice doubles in quantity and then, hey presto, turns into water.

MAGIC
WITH LIQUIDS

The Hydrostatic Tube

The magician shows an unprepared glass tube. A piece of paper is torn into two and one piece placed over one end of the tube. The magician fills the tube with water and places the remaining half of the paper on top. When the hand is removed from the lower piece of paper, the water remains in the tube. This, it is explained, is simply air pressure keeping the paper in place. Now for the magic: the magician, having already removed the lower paper, goes on to remove the upper paper and still the water remains inside – a miracle! The papers are replaced, and the magician takes the hatpin and holds the tube over the bowl. The upper paper is pierced with the pin, the action being held for a second or two, and then the pin is withdrawn with the paper impaled upon it. The water gushes out into the bowl, taking the lower paper with it.

This is one of David Devant's great masterpieces. He usually followed it with 'Wine and Water' (see page 196) as the preparation necessary for the second trick helped him with the first.

If you plan to follow up with 'The Wine and Water Trick', you must make the following preparations. Place a tray on your table and arrange four glass tumblers upon it. Reading from the left, the second and fourth tumblers are inverted. Behind the glasses there is a large glass tube with a piece of paper tucked into one end, a finger bowl with two spouts containing water, and a large hatpin.

For 'The Hydrostatic Tube' you will also require two small discs of glass which fit over the ends of the tube. The ends themselves must be ground perfectly level and the discs must be rebated, i.e. they must have a shoulder all around their circumferences. When placed on the ends of the tube, they must not be able to move laterally. One of the discs must also have a tiny hole drilled through its centre (Fig. 1). The hole is filled with a piece of moistened soap at the start of the trick. The soap must be soft so always complete this part of the preparation just before the performance.

In the days of 'The Yellow Perils', the tube would be a glass lamp chimney and the discs would also be made of glass, as described. Nowadays both tube and discs can be of perspex, not only making their manufacture so much easier but also making their transportation much safer. And, of course, it is not necessary to go hunting for a finger bowl; a large glass jug is quite satisfactory.

Before you start, place the disc with the hole in it on top of the fourth tumbler and the ordinary disc on the second tumbler. Begin the trick by showing the tube and rattling the hatpin inside it to prove that it is unprepared. Put the tube down, take up the sheet of paper, and tear it down the centre. Place one half of the paper on the fourth tumbler, over the disc with the hole. Immerse the second piece of paper in the bowl of water and lay it on top of the second tumbler. Take the paper from the fourth tumbler, wet it, and return it.

Both pieces of paper are now wet and positioned over the discs. Pick up the paper on the second tumbler, plus the disc secretly underneath it, and place them on top of the tube, taking great care not to let the disc talk against the tube. Holding both disc and paper in place, invert the tube, and fill it completely full of water. Now pick up the other piece of paper with the disc hidden beneath it and place them on top of the tube. The pieces of wet paper should be moulded round the tube so helping to conceal the discs.

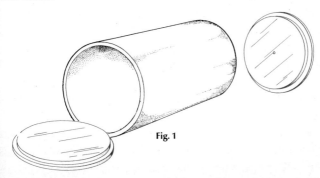

Fig. 1

Turn the tube over, bringing the disc with the hole to the bottom. Give the disc a press to ensure that it is held securely by suction. Remove your hand and it will appear as if the water is being held in the tube merely by air pressure. Next, hold the tube at its centre and slowly remove the lower piece of paper, placing it between your lips while you proceed to remove the upper paper. Pretend to be nervous at this point, which shouldn't be difficult. Hold the tube absolutely still so the spectators can fully comprehend the magnitude of the miracle they are witnessing. The tube is full of water yet there is nothing to hold it in at top or bottom!

Now place the paper that was on top of the tube over the lower end and mould it round the tube. Take the second piece of paper from your lips and mould it around the upper end of the tube. Turn the tube around again, bringing the disc with the hole to the top once more. Pick up the hatpin and pierce the upper paper, making sure that it passes through the hole in the disc unimpeded by the piece of soap.

Remove the pin, letting the air in and causing the water to fall into the bowl, taking the lower disc and paper with it. Immediately replace the pin once the water is flowing. Remove the pin again but this time also take the disc and paper impaled upon it and push these off the pin into the bowl. Allow the disc to float to the bottom, where it will land on top of the disc already there. Remove both papers from the bowl and you will now be able to hold it up for all to see that there is 'nothing' in it to explain the mystery. Show the glass tube once more, rattle the hatpin inside it, and go on to your next trick.

The Famous Wine and Water Trick

This is a perfect illustration of the saying 'It's not what you do, but the way that you do it.' 'The Wine and Water' effect is just a simple chemical experiment but, in the right hands, it becomes a miracle. Many master magicians have included it in their performances, even David Devant, and it is his version I give here.

Four glass tumblers are used, together with a glass jug of water. The magician pours a little water into one glass and returns it to the jug. Then each of the glasses is half filled, but to everyone's surprise, although the liquid in the first and third glasses is obviously water, the second and fourth glasses contain wine! The magician takes up the first and second glasses and mixes the contents together. The result is one glass full of wine, and when the wine is poured into the jug all the water it contains instantly turns to wine too. The contents of the third and fourth glasses are mixed together, but this time the result is a glass of clear water. This is poured into the jug and all becomes clear water again.

As I have already admitted, the effect is brought about chemically. Whenever dealing with chemicals great care must be taken because they can be poisonous, as in this case. Also, from a performing point of view, chemicals react differently in the water of different districts. Therefore you must always try a trick out first to determine the correct quantities to use.

Prepare the glasses by putting a teaspoonful of a saturated solution of tannin in the first glass, a few drops of a saturated solution of perchloride of iron ('steel drops') in the second and fourth glasses, and a few drops of a saturated solution of oxalic acid in the third glass. The jug contains ordinary water.

Once you have poured a little water into the first glass and back into the jug, you should proceed with the trick fairly quickly as the tannin/water mix will start to go cloudy. If you follow the routine as described above, the chemicals will do the rest. At the conclusion of the trick, the jug should be removed at once as the 'water' will quickly become dull and cloudy. This liquid is poisonous so the jug and glasses should be washed out thoroughly as soon as possible.

It is a nice touch to have the second and fourth tumblers upside down at the beginning to 'prove' that they are empty. To do this, you simply rinse the steel drops round these tumblers just before you go on.

The Passe-Passe Bottle and Glass

Many comedy versions of this very old trick have been produced, often revealing the *modus operandi*. Nevertheless, when performed properly, it is still a worthwhile effect, capable of mystifying an audience.

A large beer bottle is shown together with a small glass tumbler and two cardboard tubes. Beer is poured from the bottle into the glass and a little of this returned to the bottle via a small funnel. The bottle is placed upon a table to the performer's left. The cardboard covers are shown empty and their function of fitting over the glass and bottle respectively is demonstrated. One cover goes over the bottle again and is left there; the second cover is placed over the glass and also left there. On completion of a few mystical passes of the hands, or the magic wand, the performer raises the covers to show that the glass is now on the right-hand table whereas the bottle has transferred to the left. The covers are then replaced, more mystical waves, and the glass and bottle return to their original places.

Of course you need two bottles and two glasses. Whereas the glasses are quite normal, the bottles are very special indeed. They are made of metal and painted to resemble beer bottles. They bear identical beer labels, and it is a good idea to tear a little off each of them to match because this helps considerably towards achieving an identical appearance. Internally, however, the bottles are quite different.

One of them is slightly larger than the other and is simply a hollow shell with no base. The other has its base fixed about halfway down, leaving room for a glass to be hidden inside the bottle beneath the base. A small metal tube runs from the mouth of this bottle, down the neck, to a hole in the base which brings it above the hidden glass. This means that you can pour liquid into the bottle quite easily or, with the aid of a funnel, down through the tube directly into the hidden glass. So that you can pick up both bottle and glass together, the bottles have small holes drilled through them at the back (Fig. 2).

At the start both glasses are empty. One is on view whereas the second is hidden inside the smaller bottle with the larger bottle over both. Show the tubes empty and demonstrate that they fit over the 'bottle' by slipping one over it. In removing the tube, press against its sides and also remove the shell bottle. Pick up the smaller bottle and, by inserting the tip of your middle finger into the hole, pick up the glass too (Fig. 3).

Pour some beer from the bottle into the visible glass, but apparently pour too much. Place the funnel in the tube at the mouth of the bottle and pour back into the hidden glass exactly half the contents of the first glass. To your audience, of course, it appears that the beer is going back

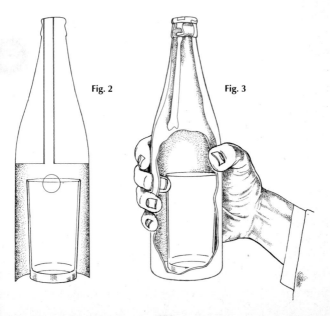

Fig. 2   Fig. 3

into the bottle. Place the glass on one table and the bottle, with the glass hidden inside, on the other. Cover the glass with the tube that already secretly contains the larger shell bottle and cover the smaller bottle with the empty tube. You are now in the position of being able to show either a bottle or a glass at will.

Simply raise the cover over the glass, leave the shell bottle behind, to show that the glass has gone and that the bottle has taken its place. Pick up the other cover, taking the smaller bottle with it, to show that the bottle has gone and the glass has flown there. Make bottle and glass change places again by reversing these moves. At the conclusion, casually drop the tube containing the shell bottle over its twin before clearing your table for the next trick.

The Rice Bowls

Along with 'The Chinese Linking Rings' and 'The Cups and Balls', 'The Rice Bowls' is one of the world's oldest tricks. Over the centuries, there have been several variations, both in method and effect. Two versions, however, have outstripped the rest for popularity and here they are. The first uses two china bowls, the second bowls of brass. The effect is the same in each case.

The magician shows two small bowls on a tray, pours a little rice into one of them, and covers it with the other bowl. Then the upper bowl is removed and the rice has increased to such an extent that it is heaped up in the lower bowl and overflowing onto the tray. The rice is levelled off flat. Now one bowl is empty whereas the other is full to the brim with rice. Again the magician puts the empty bowl on top of the rice-filled one and, on removal, it is found that all the rice has disappeared and in its place – water! This is poured from bowl to bowl as the audience applaud a very clever Eastern mystery.

The china-bowl method First, let us look at the version which requires two china bowls of identical size. One of these has its edge ground perfectly flat. You will also need a circular disc of perspex of the same size as the top of each bowl, its circumference being ground down to produce a shoulder. This will help ensure a tight fit on the prepared bowl.

Fill one bowl to the brim with water. Wet the edge of the bowl and also the shoulder of the disc with water. Press the disc onto the bowl, making sure that it is flush all the way round. In this condition it should be possible to turn the bowl upside down with no risk of the water pouring out. If the disc is made with care, you should even be able to toss the bowl into the air without fear. Make sure that the exposed surface of the disc is perfectly dry and place it upside down on two matchsticks on the tray. This will ensure that the disc does not adhere to the tray and ruin the whole proceedings. Place the empty bowl upside down over the prepared bowl. You will also need on the tray a bag of rice.

Show the empty bowl, half fill it with rice, and stand it on the tray. Pick up the prepared bowl and place it 'mouth to mouth' on top of the first bowl. Make sure that they fit exactly together. Using both your hands, one either side, pick up the bowls, reverse them, and put them down again. Now the prepared bowl is underneath. The rice will fall on top of the perspex disc and, when you remove the upper bowl, it will appear to have more than doubled in quantity.

With a series of scooping movements using the empty bowl, gradually push more and more of the rice off the fake onto the tray. When the fake is almost uncovered, get a fingernail under it and, in apparently pushing off more rice, very quickly slide the disc off the bowl onto the tray (Fig. 4). It will fall unnoticed amongst the rice. As soon as the disc is off, cover the bowl that contains water with the empty bowl again. Lift the upper bowl off in your right hand, pick up the lower bowl in your left hand, and pour the water from bowl to bowl.

At the start of the trick, you are of course able to show

only one bowl empty. This is a weakness in the trick but how important a weakness is a matter for personal assessment. Some magicians would argue that, as the bowl is held upside down, it 'must be empty'. On the other hand, it could be claimed that it is the magician's duty to eradicate all weaknesses.

The obvious way is to switch in the prepared bowl. If you decide to take this course, you will need three bowls. First show the two unprepared bowls to be quite empty, and then switch one for the prepared bowl. This can be done in several different ways.

For instance, if your bag of rice is large enough to hide a bowl, this could be used as a cover. Show the bowls, one in each hand, and put them down, the left one first but then, almost simultaneously, the right one. You apparently find, however, that there is little room on the small tray so you are forced to place the right-hand bowl behind the bag of rice. In fact you lower it straight down onto a servante – in this case a small shelf fixed to the back of the table – and immediately bring your right hand up again to the prepared

Fig. 4

disc

bowl. At this point, lift the bag of rice out of the way with your left hand and the switch has been accomplished. With practice you will be able to perform this manoeuvre quite undetected by your audience.

If you are performing close up, it is better to have the rice in a box rather than a bag. With very small rice bowls it is a simple matter indeed to switch the bowls. With the prepared bowl in the box, hold an empty bowl in each hand and proceed to dip them into the box and bring them out full of rice. Empty both bowls into the box and then repeat the exercise. On the third go, you must leave one of the bowls behind and bring out the prepared bowl instead. It is essential that you make the change in one continuous move so as not to arouse suspicion. Constant practice is the only answer. You tip the prepared bowl upside down as though pouring back the rice once more. Then take both bowls from the box, and place them face down on the tray, the gimmicked one going on the matches. Pick up the unprepared bowl, half fill it with rice, and proceed with the trick. You could close the lid of the box and use it as a table.

The brass-bowl method Using brass bowls, you do not need a perspex disc, nor is it necessary to switch bowls. One of the bowls is specially manufactured to work the trick yet both bowls can be shown completely empty with their interiors towards the audience. Obviously this is a big improvement upon the first method.

The special bowl has an inner lining, leaving sufficient space between it and the bowl itself to hold a considerable quantity of water. Like the rest of the bowl, the lining is of highly polished brass and can be shown to the audience with impunity, provided it is kept moving. Near the top edge of the faked bowl, there is a small airhole, and another is positioned at the centre of the bottom of the 'outer' bowl.

To fill the space between the lining and the 'outer' bowl with water and keep it inside until you are ready, carry out

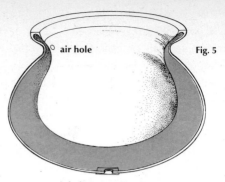

air hole

Fig. 5

air hole covered by plaster

the following procedure. Immerse the bowl in water. Hold it there until no more bubbles of air appear. As you lift the bowl out of the water, put a finger over the airhole near the brim because with this hole closed the water will not escape from the bottom hole. Dry the bowl thoroughly, still keeping your finger tightly over the hole, and then, with a small piece of rubber plaster, seal the bottom hole (Fig. 5). Now you can turn the bowl upside down, happy in the knowledge that the water will not escape from the airhole near the brim. Thoroughly dry the inside of the bowl and all is ready for the performance.

As before, the tray is set with the fake bowl mouth downwards and the ordinary bowl on top of it. Pick up the ordinary bowl in your left hand and the special bowl in your right hand and show them face on to the audience. Half fill the ordinary bowl with rice and put the special bowl on top of it. Often the bowls are designed almost to clip together. Invert the two bowls and remove the upper bowl, now the ordinary one, and the rice will appear to have increased due to the much smaller interior of the special bowl.

As there is no disc to get rid of, it is not necessary to use the ordinary bowl as a scoop. Instead level off the rice with your hand in full view and, under cover of the other bowl as you are about to put it on top again, quickly scoop out with your fingers as much of the rice as possible (Fig. 6). It doesn't matter if a little remains, but the audience must not be aware that you are emptying the bowl. As far as the spectators are concerned, it is filled with rice to the brim. Complete the action of covering the special bowl and then invert both. Before setting them down on the table again, secretly remove the adhesive rubber plaster from the airhole in the bottom of the bowl, thus enabling the water to flow through the second airhole at the brim into the ordinary bowl.

This is where the snag comes in. I have already pointed out the improvements on the china-bowl method; now I must point out the drawback. It takes all of a minute for the water to run from the inner compartment of the special bowl, through the airhole, and out into the ordinary bowl underneath.

If you are used to pattering, this isn't too big a problem, but a minute is a long time on a stage. If you perform silently, it is necessary to introduce another smaller, but complementary, trick at this stage to pass the time away. Nevertheless many performers prefer this method and have found ways of overcoming the problem.

Once the water has run into the lower bowl, you can pick up both bowls and even apparently increase the amount of water by pouring it back into the fake bowl, finally tipping it into a glass jug.

Fig. 6

The Indian Sands

Whenever I meet elderly people, I try to get them to re-member the magicians they saw in their youth. In this way, I have had first-hand descriptions of some of the greatest magic acts of all time. I met a man who had been a mechanic working for Maskelyne and Devant at the St George's Hall in London. I also knew a man who had been an electrician at London's old Hotel Cecil and had taken part in the acts of such great magicians as Houdini himself. Only a week or so ago, I asked an elderly gentleman to cast his mind back to his childhood and try to recall the trick that he found most mysterious. He said, 'The trick with the coloured sand', and proceeded to describe the wonderful effect that follows.

The magician shows a large glass bowl and allows it to be thoroughly examined. Next the bowl is filled with ordinary water from a large glass jug. Showing the left hand un-doubtedly empty, the magician picks up a bag with the right hand and pours into the left hand a large quantity of red sand, a little at a time. Nothing is concealed in either hand, nor is anything other than sand poured from the bag. The sand is then tipped into the bowl and the water is coloured red. Next the magician takes a bag of white or natural sand and treats it in exactly the same way, and finally a bag of blue sand. Throughout it is made very clear that nothing is concealed in either of the hands and only sand is poured from the bags. The water is now completely coloured.

The magician rolls up his or her sleeves, plunges the empty right hand into the water, and brings it out contain-ing a handful of wet sand. This is put back and the hand is shown empty again. Once more the magician dips the right hand into the bowl and takes it out closed. A glass goblet is picked up with the left hand and held under the closed right hand, from which dry red sand slowly trickles. When the hand is completely empty, the magician opens it and shows it to the audience. The goblet is put down, the hands are washed, the performance is repeated with the white and later the blue sand. At the conclusion of the trick, there for all to see are three clear glass goblets containing perfectly dry red, white, and blue sand. The water and its sludge can be poured into another receptacle and everything examined.

The best tricks are brought about by the simplest means, and this is one of them. But it is only right to voice a warning. Although the method is simple and its performance easy, to put this into the miracle class, as achieved by the master magicians, a very high standard of showmanship is essential.

The main secret of the method lies in the special preparation of small quantities of the three different coloured sands. The first job is to dye quantities of white or natural sand red and blue. The next is to put a small amount of the white or natural sand into an old frying pan and heat it until it is extremely hot. Then drop a small lump of tallow candle into the pan and stir it well into the sand, covering every grain, when it has melted. This done, remove the pan from the heat, take out the sand, and mould it. Repeat this operation with the red and blue sands. As it is necessary to know by feel the colour of the sand in the mould you hold, the material must be fashioned into three different and easily recognizable shapes: one for the white sand, one for the red, and one for the blue. When the moulds cool, they go hard and are waterproof.

Use paper bags to hold the sand. Turn a bag upside down and push the bottom up into the bag, making room for the moulds. Put two or three moulds of one colour in the bottom of each bag, and then fill the bags with the corresponding coloured sand (Fig. 7).

Care must be taken when lifting the bags to keep the moulds in the cavities at the bottom by means of your little finger. In my opinion, the best way to get the moulds into the bowl is as follows. As in the description of the effect, pour the sand into your empty left hand, holding it over the

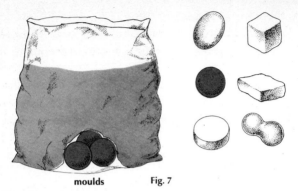

moulds   **Fig. 7**

bowl because some of the sand is certain to fall off. Now
trickle the sand into the bowl a little at a time but end up
with quite a flow. Under cover of this flow, simply remove
your right little finger from the bottom of the bag and allow
the moulds to drop in under cover of the sand flowing from
your other hand.

When working on a stage with the audience some distance away, it would be possible to place the moulds actually in the bags and take them out with your hand, putting
them in under cover of the loose sand. No doubt under
those conditions one could get away with it, but it does not
make for the clear-cut presentation that is so essential to
the effectiveness of this trick. As already stated, the key to
success here lies entirely in showmanship and careful
handling. It is essential that the audience is convinced at
every stage that there is no deception, failing this the trick
will fall completely flat.

To return to the routine. First take out a handful of the
wet mixed sand to show the audience that it is just that –
wet and mixed. This emphasizes the magnitude of the task
before you. Now dip your hand into the bowl and bring
out a handful of the appropriate moulds in turn, crush them
in your hand, and pour out the dry sand into the three
goblets.

You may find some grease floating on top of the water at the conclusion of this trick. If you are performing in a drawing room, or anywhere else where the audience is close to you, it is as well to empty the water away at the earliest opportunity.

Several other methods have been devised to bring about this great effect. None in my opinion comes up to this one.

The Dissolved Card

The magician has a card freely selected and marked. It is placed under a handkerchief and then the handkerchief, with the card in its folds, is held over a jug of clear water while the card is dropped into the jug. On removing the handkerchief, the card is seen to have dissolved and completely disappeared. The magician picks up two small slates and wipes them clean, using water from the jug and a small sponge. Placing the slates together, the magician then wraps them in a sheet of newspaper and gives them to someone to hold. The audience probably imagines that the name of the chosen card is going to appear in chalk upon one of the slates. Not so however. When the slates are unwrapped, the actual chosen, marked card is seen to be between them.

The secret of this trick lies in a neat combination of subtle but easy moves and a special gimmick. This consists of a piece of transparent plastic exactly the same size as a card. At the start of the trick, the gimmick is lying on your table, hidden by a large handkerchief or scarf. You will also need a large glass jug filled with water, a sponge, and a pack of cards.

Shuffle the cards, keeping their faces towards the spectators so they can see that it is an ordinary pack. Have one card selected by the fairest means possible as it really does not matter which is chosen. Ask for the card to be marked and placed on top of the pack. Drop the pack face upwards on your table behind the handkerchief and directly over the plastic gimmick.

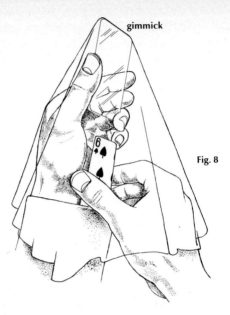

gimmick

Fig. 8

Immediately pick up the handkerchief and show it to be unprepared. Next pick up the pack and the gimmick, turn them over so that the cards are face downwards, and take off the top chosen card, together with the gimmick. You will have to practise this move. You may find it easier to slide the gimmick a little way off the pack first, then do the same with the chosen card, and pick them up together. Place the cards, as one, into your left hand, taking care to hold them with your fingers on the left-hand side and your thumb on the right.

Throw the handkerchief over the card(s). Once both are covered, push the gimmick card upwards with your left forefinger. Put your right hand inside the handkerchief as if to arrange it with its centre over the 'card'. While your right hand is under the handkerchief, take the chosen card and push it into your left sleeve (Fig. 8). Remove your right hand, bring it over the top of the handkerchief, and take hold of the gimmick card. Ask someone to hold it over the jug and drop it at the word 'go'. This done, you remove the handkerchief to show that the card has dissolved completely. The transparent gimmick card has sunk to the bottom and become invisible.

Now comes a move which requires practice. You pick up both slates, dip the sponge into the jug of water, and clean the side that faces the audience. Turn this slate over and wash the other side. Next change the position of the slates: grasp them in your right hand near to where they are resting on your left hand and, under cover of the slates, pop your first and second fingers into your left sleeve, withdraw the card, and hold it against the back slate. Now take the slates in your left hand at the nearside edges and slide out the back one, leaving the card pressed against the rear of the front slate. Bring the back slate to the front and clean it. Turn it over and clean the other side. Holding the card against the back slate with your left fingers, take the front slate in your right hand, and once more place it behind the other one, bringing the card between the two.

Wrap the slates up in a piece of newspaper and hand them to someone to hold. Suddenly remember that you used water from the jug in which the chosen card dissolved and say that this might have some effect on the outcome of the slate trick. Ask the spectator to unwrap the slates and the marked card is revealed.

The Vanishing Glass of Water

Here are three ways of vanishing a glass of liquid. It need not be water; in fact a coloured liquid like wine helps to dress the trick up a bit. The effect is the same in each case. The magician part fills a glass tumbler with liquid and covers it with a handkerchief. The shape of the glass is clearly seen, proving that the glass is indeed inside the handkerchief. Then, well away from the table or any other apparatus, the magician gives the handkerchief a shake and the glass of liquid completely disappears.

All three methods require a gimmick which consists of a circular disc of cardboard sewn into the handkerchief. A deluxe model can be made by sewing two handkerchiefs together with the disc between them.

First method   This can be performed seated at a table. You part fill the tumbler from a jug and cover it with the gimmicked handkerchief so that the hidden disc rests exactly on its mouth. You now appear to pick up the glass through the handkerchief with your right hand. What you actually do, however, is take only the disc between the tips of your fingers and thumb and raise this together with the handkerchief. At the same time, you place your left hand under the handkerchief, ostensibly to steady the glass, and calmly lower it onto your lap. Then you replace your left hand under the handkerchief. With practice you will be able to perform this movement, completely covered by the handkerchief, without arousing your audience's suspicions at all.

Raise the supposed tumbler high off the table, shake the handkerchief, and quickly open it so that it hangs flat with your forefingers and thumbs at each of the two upper corners. The glass has vanished. When the glass is on your lap, grip it between your thighs to make sure that it does not fall over. From this position it can be subsequently loaded into a hat for reproduction.

Second method   Although very similar to the first method, this one can be worked standing up and is therefore suitable for performance on a platform or stage. In addition to the gimmicked handkerchief, the liquid in a jug, and the glass tumbler, you will need a servante, in this case a small shelf that fits on the rear of a table.

Perform exactly as for the first method but, instead of lowering the glass onto your lap, you secretly set it down on the servante.

Third method   This is probably the best as it does away with the necessity of removing the glass from the handkerchief with your left hand. Once again you need the

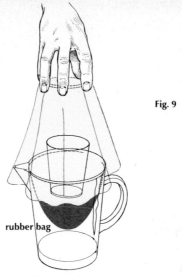

Fig. 9

rubber bag

gimmick sewn in a handkerchief, a glass tumbler, and a jug of liquid. This time, however, the jug is not all that it seems. It has been fitted with a rubber bag, which holds the liquid in the first place but is emptied on filling the tumbler.

Again the glass is covered by the gimmicked handkerchief but with this method, when the gimmick is picked up by the tips of your right fingers and thumb, you pick up the glass as well. To prove to the audience that the glass is still under the handkerchief, you tap it against the top of the jug but, unknown to the audience, you then release the glass and allow it to fall into the rubber bag (Fig. 9). The glass, of course, still appears to be under the handkerchief because the disc conveys that impression.

Another vanishing glass trick

Although this is yet another way of vanishing a glass of liquid, it is so different from the first three that it deserves a separate explanation. The magician pours liquid into a clear glass tumbler and covers it with a small cardboard tube. On raising the tube, the magician reveals that the liquid has completely disappeared.

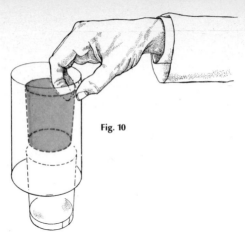

Fig. 10

For this one you will need a glass tumbler fitted with a clear plastic lining and a cardboard tube of such a size as to fit loosely over the glass.

The working of this effect is extremely simple. With the lining in place quite undetected by the audience, pour some liquid into the glass and cover it with the tube. To make the liquid disappear, simply remove the tube from the glass, fingers inside, thumb on the outside, using its cover simultaneously to whisk the lining away (Fig. 10). Seeing that the liquid has gone, the audience will have good reason to wish to inspect the cardboard cover. It is necessary therefore to have a black-art well in your table and to place the tube over this, so lowering the glass into it out of sight. Then you can pick up the tube and show it empty.

Vanishing a glass of liquid is not a complete trick in itself but it could easily become part of a more complex routine. For instance, instead of liquid one could put silk handkerchiefs into the glass and make everything disappear only to reproduce the silks from someone's coat pocket and the glass from someone's hat.

The Tube of Aquarius

Several years ago I attended a sale of secondhand apparatus at the famous Magic Circle in London. Amongst the

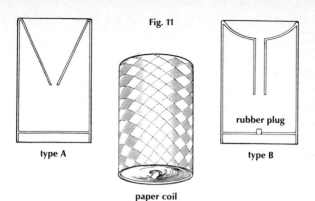

Fig. 11

type A

rubber plug

type B

paper coil

treasures I purchased was a box of gimmicks which included the Tube of Aquarius, the gimmick necessary for the performance of the following trick.

The magician shows a piece of stiff paper on both sides and rolls it into a tube. Water is then poured into one end and the audience is surprised to see that it does not immediately shoot out at the other, but remains suspended inside. Then, reaching up inside the tube, the magician begins to produce a large quantity of paper ribbons of all the colours of the rainbow and all perfectly dry. As a result the table is covered in a whole mound of them. On opening the paper tube, the magician shows that it is quite empty and unprepared in any way.

I have already mentioned that a special gimmick is involved. This consists of a metal tube constructed like an unspillable inkwell. Originally, it was made like Type A (Fig. 11) but, as this was difficult to empty, it was later modified to Type B, which has a hole in the base closed with a rubber plug during performance. The floor of the gimmick is not fixed flush with the lower end of the tube, but is high enough to allow space for a coil of paper ribbon. A very important feature of the metal gimmick is its outside appearance. It must be decorated to match the ribbons; in other words it is camouflaged.

To begin the trick, hold one end of the square of stiff paper in your left hand, thumb at the front, fingers at the back. Unknown to the audience, you also have the gimmick held in those fingers. Take the lower end of the paper in your right hand, bring it up to your left thumb, and hold it under this. At the same moment release the top edge of the paper from under your left thumb and let it fall down naturally. By this means you have shown both sides of the paper but managed to keep the gimmick hidden behind it. Now, using both hands, roll up the paper with the gimmick inside. Then hold it with your left hand at its lower end, your little finger extended to ensure that the gimmick does not fall out.

Pour a little water into the top of the paper tube and thereby into the gimmick. Hold the tube steady for a moment to let the audience realize that the water has remained inside. Then, with the forefinger and thumb of your left hand, reach underneath and start the ribbon unwinding from the centre. Once started, the coil will unwind of its own volition until a large mound is formed on your table. To ditch the gimmick, simply lower the tube of paper until it touches the top of the mound and release the metal tube so that it falls unseen, due to its camouflage, amongst the paper ribbons.

It is a good idea to pull the centre of the coil out a little before you start to avoid fumbling during the performance. Before loading the gimmick, the outer ribbon of the coil should be broken, or you will find the last little piece of the ribbon will be a ring of paper, which will look suspicious to any curious spectator.

It is an easy matter to turn this trick into a grand finale if you wish by producing the 'flags of all nations' from the ribbons. To do this, make a neat bundle of the flags, securing them with a piece of thread to which a wire loop has been attached, and hide them in a black-art well. Just pick up a bunch of the ribbons, secretly hooking up the bundle with them, break the thread, and make your big production.

Water from Paper

The magician shows a box full of paper shavings. He or she takes a small plastic cup, plunges it into the box, and brings it out full to overflowing. The shavings are tipped back and the cup is filled once more. Then the magician takes a small handkerchief and covers the cup for a moment. When the handkerchief is removed, the cup is discovered full to the brim with water. This is tipped out into a jug and the cup is passed round for examination.

You will need two similar plastic cups and a rubber cap to fit one of the cups. This can be obtained from most magic-dealers. To prepare, you must glue paper shavings onto the rubber cap until it is completely covered. Fill one of the cups with liquid and seal it by putting on the rubber cap. Hide this prepared cup under the paper shavings in the box.

First show the unprepared cup, scoop up some shavings from the box, and tip them back again. Appear to do this once more but in reality switch it for the prepared cup. Bring this cup out of the box with a few loose shavings on the top, brush these off, and cover with the handkerchief. On removing the handkerchief, secretly pull off the rubber cap as well and the water can be revealed.

The Coffee Vase

This elegant piece of apparatus was considered old when 'The Yellow Perils' were published but, as the dealers are offering such pieces for sale again, perhaps it is due for a comeback.

The magician shows a beautiful metal vase to be empty and proceeds to fill it with cotton wool. The vase is covered with a cardboard tube but this is discarded when the trick appears to fail. With cotton wool still filling the vase, the magician places a small lid on top. After a few mystic waves, the lid is removed and hot coffee is poured out.

The tall, straight-sided vase has a foot and is usually made of chromed metal. It also has a special metal lining, quite separate from the vase, with its own outer sheath and this, when fitted over the vase, does not alter the latter's appearance in any way. The container section of the lining does not extend to the bottom of the vase when it is in place, and it has a little metal cup positioned inside the top of the container and a metal lid that fits closely inside the secret cup (Fig. 12). You also need a tube of cardboard which goes snugly over the lining.

Prepare by filling the secret cup with cotton wool and the lining with hot coffee. Position the secret cup at the top of the lining. Make sure that the cotton wool is packed well down out of sight. Position the lining over the vase.

Show the tube empty and demonstrate that it goes over the vase. As you remove the tube from the vase, take with it the lining. Now show the vase empty and fill it with cotton wool. Cover the vase with the tube once more, so returning the lining. Look into the top of the tube and say that the trick doesn't seem to be working. Put your fingers into the top and pull the small piece of cotton wool in the secret cup up a little so that, when you remove the tube, it will be seen. Say that the trick can't have worked as the cotton wool is still there. Now pick up the metal lid and place it on top. Try some magic words, remove the lid, taking the secret cup with it, and you are able to pour out the coffee.

Fig. 12

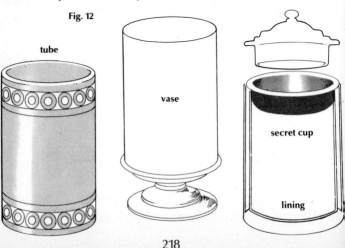

tube

vase

secret cup

lining

218

The Big, Big Finish

When I was a boy, I used to go to the music hall practically every week, especially, of course, if the bill included a magic act. One act I saw on many occasions was that of Kardoma. With his well-known billing 'He fills the stage with flags', Kardoma was in great demand as a 'closer'. This final item in my chapter on liquid magic is also a very suitable finish.

The magician shows a large cylinder to be empty and proceeds to fill it with water. Then, plunging both hands inside, he or she produces flag upon flag until the stage is covered in them. The water is poured out of the cylinder again and, just when the audience bursts into applause for what it thinks is the end of the trick, the magician produces a huge Stars and Stripes, Union Jack, or some other appropriate national flag.

The method and apparatus for this trick are extremely simple. It relies solely upon the colourful spectacle of so many flags filling the stage for its effect. The cylinder has a central compartment sealed off from the water by a rubber cap (Fig. 13). All the flags are concealed inside this compartment except the final national flag, which has a button sewn to each of its upper two corners and is hidden behind the back of a chair. The handling of this trick is greatly aided if you have the services of an assistant to

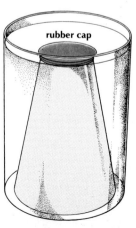

rubber cap

Fig. 13

hold the cylinder while you fill it to the brim with water.

The construction of the cylinder only allows for a quick flash of the interior when showing it empty. Keep it moving in a long sweep as you hold the opening towards the audience. Fill the cylinder from a jug, remove the rubber cap, hiding it in the folds of the first flag you produce, and proceed to drape the tables and chairs on the stage with flags. Make sure you put some over the chair behind which the finale flag is hidden.

When the flags have all been removed from the cylinder, pour out the water and take your applause. As this starts to wane, pick up the few flags from the special chair, together with the hidden finale flag, take one end yourself (the button will help here) and have your assistant take the other. Walking smartly away from each other, rapidly develop the flag to 'bring the house down'.

APPENDICES

The Magic Masters

The Father of Modern Magic

Back in 1805 in Blois, France, on 7 December was born a man who was destined to change the face of magic. His professional name was Robert-Houdin. He first appeared in Paris in 1845 with an act that completely dispensed with the draped tables and gaudy 'props' normally used by the magicians of the day. Houdin was a favourite with royalty and performed for King Louis Philippe of France and Queen Victoria of England. He died on 13 June, 1871.

Maskelyne and Cooke

From 1873 to 1934 the focal point of the magic scene in England was Maskelyne's Mysteries. The founder, John Nevil Maskelyne, was born in Cheltenham, England, on 22 December, 1839. Together with his friend George Alfred Cooke, in 1865 he exposed the Davenport Brothers, fraudulent mediums from America, and duplicated their so-called spiritualist performance. In 1869 Maskelyne and Cooke entertained the Prince of Wales.

In 1873 they leased a theatre in the Egyptian Hall, Piccadilly, London. Originally built to house William Bullock's 16,000 natural wonders, the Egyptian Hall was being used as a place of unusual entertainments: automata, second-sight, manikins, and the like. It was decorated with sphinxes, scarabs, and hieroglyphics and was used by such performers as the great Alexander Herrmann, Colonel Stodare, and Dr Lynn.

Maskelyne invented the famous box escape that was later used by Houdini.

In August 1893 David Devant joined the company. Devant, born David Wighton in Holloway, London, on 22

EGYPTIAN HALL, PICCADILLY.
EVERY EVENING AT EIGHT
Every Monday, Wednesday, and Saturday, at Three.

Commencing MONDAY EVENING, May 26th, and continuing throughout the Season.

Be sure you ask for Maskelyne & Cooke's Tickets, and see that you get them—Second Pay Box from Piccadilly Entrance, situated on the first floor, & not on the basement

MASKELYNE AND COOKE
THE ROYAL ILLUSIONISTS, AND THEIR
LONDON COMPANY

Amongst other Marvellous Illusions there will be the Extraordinary Phenomenon of

A LADY FLOATING IN THE AIR.

SPECIAL ENGAGEMENT OF

MR. HENRY COLLARD
THE POCKET SIMS REEVES

Who created such a furore in the Pantomimes at Drury Lane in 1871 and 1872. This clever little Artiste is less than Tom Thumb, and his singing has been eulogized by the entire Press of London and New York.

ROARS OF LAUGHTER AND DEAFENING APPLAUSE ARE PRODUCED BY THE

MYSTIC FREAKS OF EYCES
IN HIS ENCHANTED DEN.

TICKETS, 5s., 3s., 2s., 1s., may be obtained at Mitchell's, 33, Old Bond Street; Hay's, Royal Exchange; Austin's Ticket Office, St. James's Hall; and at the Egyptian Hall, where a Plan may be seen and Fauteuils booked from Ten till Five each day.
W. MORTON, Lessee and Manager.

STAFFORD AND CO., PRINTERS, NOTTINGHAM.

February, 1868, was a brilliant showman and an astute businessman. He invented many new illusions and the company prospered.

Maskelyne and Devant

The Egyptian Hall was closed in 1905 and the company moved to St George's Hall, Langham Place, as Maskelyne and Devant's Mysteries.

John Nevil Maskelyne died on 18 May, 1917, his son Nevil taking his place. David Devant died on 12 October, 1941. *The Times* called him 'The greatest magician of all times'. It is interesting to note that he was first bitten by the magic bug while reading Professor Hoffmann's *Modern Magic*.

Party pioneer

Charles Bertram, real name James Bassett, performed many times at Maskelyne's from 1885. He was also a pioneer of conjuring at private parties for Society and performed twenty-two times before Edward VII.

Devant's understudy

Paul Valadon was of German origin. He stood in for Devant at the Egyptian Hall while his mentor toured in 1900. He left Maskelyne's in 1904 to join the greatest American illusionist of that time, Kellar.

A new sleight

Howard Thurston was born in Columbia, Ohio, USA, in 1869. His first act consisted only of card tricks, Thurston having recognized the possibilities of the then new sleight back-palming. He added big illusions in 1900 and six years later joined Kellar. On Kellar's retirement, Thurston took over and became America's top magician.

Magic with coins

T. Nelson Downs, the first and greatest 'King of Coins', was born on 26 March, 1867, in Montour, Iowa, USA. At thirty-

The Egyptian Hall in London's Piccadilly, home of the fabulous Maskelyne family and birthplace of modern magic in England. This famous hall of entertainments closed down in 1905, unlike Jacksons, grocers to royalty.

one he was reputedly the highest-paid American variety performer. 'The Miser's Dream' made him, or perhaps it is fairer to say that he made 'The Miser's Dream'.

The Handcuff King

Undoubtedly the greatest name in American magic is that of Harry Houdini. Born Ehrich Weiss in Budapest, Hungary, on 24 March, 1874, he was taken to Appleton, Wisconsin, USA, as a child. Like Devant, his introduction to magic was via a book – *The Memoirs of Robert-Houdin* – hence Houdini. He first made his name with escapology as 'The Handcuff King'. But in 1918 he vanished an elephant in an evening show devoted entirely to illusions and became dubbed 'The Master Magician'. Houdini died on 31 October, 1926.

Supreme manipulator

The best known of all manipulators was Cardini. Born Richard Valentine Pitchford in Mumbles, Wales, on 24 November, 1899, he worked as manager of the magic department in Gamages, a London store. Emigrating to Australia and then to America, he first performed in New York with cards and cigarettes in 1926. Cardini was imitated but unequalled.

Magic today

Magic may well be entering another golden era with the return of the big illusion shows. My own full evening show, *It Must Be Magic*, includes all the old favourites like 'Sawing a Woman in Half' and 'The Floating Lady', together with many of the tricks and routines described in this book. With the closure of the variety (vaudeville) theatres, the big shows play in civic halls, school assembly-halls, church halls, and wherever enough room and an audience can be found. Magic has also found many other outlets. It can be seen on television and in clubs of every description; close-up performers 'work the tables' in restaurants and bars, at holiday camps and on cruises, while others use magic to promote new products to salesmen and customers. There are more magic clubs and magic-dealers today than ever before. This technological twentieth century has done nothing to quench our delight in the power of illusion.

FROM THE CRYSTAL PALACE, SYDENHAM

ST. JAMES'S GREAT HALL,
REGENT STREET AND PICCADILLY. FOR A LIMITED NUMBER OF REPRESENTATIONS, COMMENCING
TUESDAY, April 1st, Morning at 3, Evening at 8. WEDNESDAY Morning only at 3. THURSDAY Morning
at 3, Evening at 8. FRIDAY Morning only at 3.—(See Newspaper Advertisements for further arrangements.)

MESSRS.

MASKELYNE & COOKE

THE ROYAL ILLUSIONISTS, assisted by a TALENTED COMPANY,
WILL HAVE THE HONOR OF GIVING THEIR ORIGINAL AND NOVEL ENTERTAINMENT, INCLUDING

WILL, THE WITCH, AND THE WATCH

A SEVEN CHARACTER SKETCH, EMBRACING THE MOST MARVELLOUS

MAGICAL TRANSFORMATIONS

EVER WITNESSED.

The Press, the Public, the Clergy, the Gentry, all agree that this is an Entertainment suitable for all Classes—it being full of genuine Amusement, and entirely
free from vulgarity.

Fauteuils, 5s.   Stalls, 3s.   Balcony, 2s.   Admission, 1s.   Children under 12 Half price, except to the 1s. Seats.
Tickets can be obtained and Seats secured at the following places:—M. PIPPELL, S. 72, Old Bond Street; HAY & REED, Exchange; and at all Mitchell's Libraries, &c., in Bond Street Hall.
For full Particulars see Small Bills and Programmes.   **W. MORTON, Lessee & Manager.**

STAFFORD AND CO., PRINTERS AND ENGRAVERS, NOTTINGHAM.

The Wisdom of the Masters

'Can conjuring be learned from books? Without doubt it can. David Devant, the greatest of British conjurers, acknowledges that his first performances were entirely based on his study of book explanations of tricks. Devant had to make a beginning and he made it with the aid of books.'
Will Goldston

'Conjuring consists in the performer's audience being led to believe that certain definite actions have been carried out before them, while they presently discover that the results of those actions are something directly contrary to any natural law. They immediately recognise that they have been deceived completely, but without knowing how or when the deception took place, for they are not fools enough, nor is it desired to make them think that the supernatural has occurred. It is thus the mind of the spectator which must be deceived.'
C. Lang Neil

'So far from feeling any reluctance towards letting the general public into the secrets of our procedure, we are most anxious to educate the public in such matters, in order that a proper understanding of our art may be disseminated among its votaries and patrons. The very best audience a skilled magician can have is one composed entirely of magicians.'
Nevil Maskelyne

'Many people have the erroneous idea that if they know how a trick is done they are quite capable of presenting it to an audience. I have always found that a very little experience will show such persons that the mere knowledge of the secret of a trick is not of much value to a beginner unless it is accompanied by some simple instructions showing him the best way of using his knowledge. No conjurer can attach too much importance to rehearsals.'
David Devant

'If I had any constructive advice to offer a young person starting out in magic it would be this: at the outset he should do as many different tricks and routines as possible before the public. By so doing he will soon discover the things he can do the best and the ones that register most strongly.'
T. Nelson Downs

'Strive at all times to reach perfection. Practice, practice, and even more practice is the key. Entertain your audiences, keep it simple, and enjoy your magic. Good luck in your endeavours to become a Master Magician.'
Jack Delvin

Some Useful Addresses

As you will already have discovered, quite a lot of apparatus and accessories have been mentioned that you won't be able to make yourself. Here is a list of magic-dealers that you might like to contact. They all publish lists or catalogues which they will be pleased to send you if you provide a large stamped and addressed envelope.

United Kingdom

L. Davenport and Company, 51 Great Russell Street, London WC 1.

Hughes House of Magic, The Grange, Willow Park, Kings Lynn, Norfolk.

International Magic Studio, 89 Clerkenwell Road, Holborn, London EC 1.

House magazine: *Magic Info* (monthly).

Supreme Magic Company, 64 High Street, Bideford, Devon.

House magazine: *Magigram* (monthly).

Supreme also publish *New Pentagram*, another monthly.

The world's only magic weekly is called *Abracadabra*. This can be purchased from the listed dealers or direct from the publisher: Goodliffe the Magician, Arden Forest Industrial Estate, Alcester, Warwickshire, England.

United States of America

Abbott's Magic Manufacturing Company, Colon, Michigan 49040.

House magazine: *Tops* (monthly).

Abracadabra Magic Shop, 280 Hamilton Street, Rahway, New Jersey 07065.

Louis Tannen Incorporated, 1540 Broadway, New York, NY 10036.

Magic Incorporated, 5082N Lincoln Avenue, Chicago, Illinois 60625.

Magic Industries Incorporated, P.O. Box 860, Madison Square Station, New York, NY 10010.

House magazine: *The Magic Magazine* (monthly).

Genii, a US monthly magazine, is available from P.O. Box 36068F, Los Angeles, California 90036.

As you progress, no doubt you will wish to mix with your fellow magicians and the best way to do this is to join a magic society. Most major cities throughout the world have at least one society and here is a list of some of the best known.

United Kingdom

British Magical Society, 173 Jockey Road, Sutton Coldfield, West Midlands.

International Brotherhood of Magicians (British Ring), 'The Wand', Ferndown, Dorset.

The Magic Circle, 84 Chenies Mews, London WC 1.

The Magicians' Club, 89 Clerkenwell Road, Holborn, London EC 1.

United States of America

International Brotherhood of Magicians (HQ), 28N Main Street, Kenton, Ohio 43326.

Society of American Magicians, Aqueduct Road, RFD2, Peekskill, NY 10566.

Bibliography

Below is a list of books recommended for further reading. A number of them are no longer in print but they should be available from public libraries or from specialist second-hand book dealers.

Complete Encyclopedia of Magic by Joseph Dunninger. Lyle Stuart, Secaucus, New Jersey, 1967. Spring Books, London, 1970.

Encyclopedia of Silk Magic (3 volumes) by Harold Rice. Silk King Studios, Cincinnati, Ohio, 1948.

Expert at the Card Table by S. W. Erdnase. First published by Powner, Chicago, in 1902. Fleming, York, Pennsylvania, 1944.

Expert Card Technique by Jean Hugard and Frederick Braue. First published by Cole, Minneapolis, North Carolina, 1940. Faber and Faber, London, 1954. Dover, New York, 1974.

Magic of the Hands by Edward Victor. Waddilove, Bradford, Yorkshire, 1937/8.

Magic with Faucett Ross by Louis Ganson. Supreme Magic, Bideford, Devon, 1975.

Routined Manipulations (2 volumes) by Louis Ganson. Unique Magic Studios, London, 1953.

The Royal Road to Card Magic by Jean Hugard. Harper, New York, 1948. Faber and Faber, London, 1949.

The Tarbell Course of Magic (a series published in 7 volumes) by Harlan Tarbell. Louis Tannen, New York: vols. 1–4 1941–5, vol. 5 1948, vol. 6 1954, vol 7 1974.

Glossary

Black-art well   This is an opening cut in the top of a table with a bag or pocket fitted beneath it. If the table-top is covered in black velvet and the pocket is made of the same material, it is invisible even quite close up. This effect is considerably reinforced if the table top is decorated with a strongly contrasting trim. The braid or ribbon should be so positioned as to cover the edges of the well (Fig. 1).

red indicates the black-art well

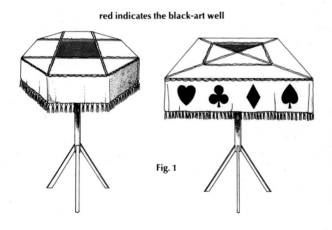

Fig. 1

Ditch   To 'ditch' something means secretly to dispose of it. A natural way to ditch, say, a ball from the palm-proper position would be to put your hand into a pocket and take out a handkerchief, leaving the ball behind. Another way is to drop the ball behind a handkerchief or piece of apparatus on your table. If your table is fitted with a black-art well or a servante, these are ideal receptacles for anything which must be ditched.

Fake   An object that appears to be quite normal in every way, but has been secretly altered to help produce a magical effect, is known as a 'fake'. In the same way, an object that has been so altered has been 'faked'. For instance, a glass tumbler which has had the bottom removed has been faked and becomes known as a fake.

Gimmick   This is the extra piece of apparatus, the extra 'something', that the audience does not see, and knows nothing about, which enables a trick to work. It can be as humble as a bit of wire or as complicated as a shortwave radio.

Load   To 'load' something is the opposite of ditching something. For instance, in 'The Tambourine Trick' it is necessary secretly to introduce the coil of paper ribbon into the tambourine. This is called 'loading'. The item being loaded is the 'load'. A good way of loading a hat with items to produce later makes use of a servante. The load is prepared by bundling up the items in a black silk tied with fine thread. Attached to the thread, there is a wire hook. Thus prepared, the load is secreted on your servante. The hat is shown empty and placed brim downwards upon the table while you roll up your sleeves. When you pick up the hat again, you hook the load onto the brim and the action of turning the hat crown downwards upon the table swings the load inside.

Pull   Similar to a vanisher, a 'pull' consists of a length of elastic or cord which can be made to pull an object rapidly out of sight or dispose of an object hidden in the palm. A form of pull is used to vanish a silk in 'The Twentieth-Century Silks Trick'. Pulls have been invented to produce many different magical effects from switching one piece of rope for another to vanishing a birdcage!

Servante   This is a secret shelf at the back of the magician's table with a 101 uses (Fig. 2). It is, of course, an ideal respository for loads prior to their being loaded (see *Load*). It is also perfect for ditching and switching. The servante can be a permanent feature of your table or you can have a portable one fitted with a G-clamp. A box placed on a card table, covered with a cloth and leaving a space at the back, also makes a serviceable servante. Yet another possibility is to use a table fitted with a drawer: just pull out the drawer a little and the job is done. Make sure your servante is covered with something soft to prevent talking.

Silks   Several tricks in this book call for the use of ordinary pocket handkerchiefs. Others are better performed with magician's handkerchiefs made of fine silk and known as 'silks'. These are essential to the success of many effects as they can be compressed into a very small compass yet, on release, rapidly expand to their full size. Silks of all sizes and all the colours of the rainbow can be obtained from magic-dealers.

Steal   To 'steal' something is secretly to obtain an object in your hand unknown to the audience. For instance, in the thimble routine it is necessary to steal five thimbles from the special holder pinned under your coat. As in ditching, a natural way to steal something without the aid of special clips or secret containers is to obtain it as you openly put something into, or take something from, a pocket.

Switch   It is often necessary in a trick secretly to change one object for another; this is called 'switching'. There are numerous examples in this book. Switches can be performed by pure sleight of hand and a perfect example of this is the 'De Manche Change'. Various pieces of apparatus

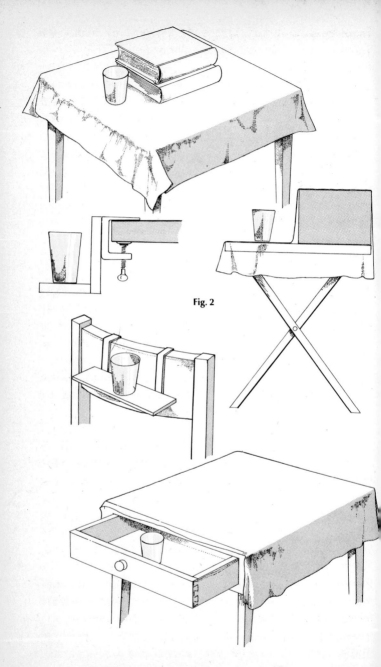

Fig. 2

have been invented to switch all sorts of things, for instance, one coin for another or a lady for a lion. A very simple and effective switch can be made using a black-art well. Have Object B on your table just in front of the well and hidden behind a silk. Show the item to be switched, Object A, and appear to place it down on the table with one hand, while removing the silk with the other. What actually happens is that undercover of the silk you drop Object A into the well a fraction of a second before lifting the silk to reveal Object B. If the action is correctly timed and performed smoothly, the spectators will not realize that the object ever left their sight.

Talking   In magician's parlance 'talking' is quite different from patter. Say, for instance, in performing the 'De Manche Change' you make a mistake and allow the coins to knock against each other, the resultant clink is known as talking. Care must be taken at all times to avoid talking as it immediately destroys any illusion. If, for instance, you are secretly lowering a glass of water under cover of a handkerchief onto your servante, and it knocks against some article already vanished, the subsequent talking will obviously give the game away.

Vanisher   As a substitute for sleight of hand, or as an alternative method in order to mislead the audience in the middle of a sleight-of-hand routine, you can use a special gimmick called a 'vanisher'. If you wish to vanish a silk, you can use a vanisher made from a hollow ball with a hole in one side and a length of elastic attached to the other. The end of the elastic is attached at the armpit inside your sleeve or to the back of your trouser waistband. During the performance, you secretly steal the hollow ball with your right hand and, when apparently pushing a silk into your closed right fist, actually push it into the vanisher. On releasing the ball, it will fly out of sight up your sleeve, or under your coat, and the silk has vanished.

Acknowledgments

With the exception of the subject on page 227, all the photographs in this book and the jacket subject were taken by Graham Portlock for the Hamlyn Publishing Group. The publishers gratefully acknowledge the generous assistance of The Magic Circle during the taking of these photographs and in particular the ever patient encouragement of Harold Frake. Our thanks also go to Francis White, the President of the Magic Circle, and to John Palfreyman, John Salisse (who also owns the photograph reproduced on page 227), Alan Snowden, Peter Warlock, and Waddingtons Playing Card Co. Ltd., who supplied the playing cards used in the illustrations.